MW01244103

Self-Directed:

Inspire, Motivate, and Empower Yourself to the Greatness That Lies Within

Connie Ragen Green

Self-Directed: Inspire, Motivate, and Empower Yourself to the Greatness That Lies Within

Connie Ragen Green

Copyright © 2023 by Hunter's Moon Publishing

ISBN Paperback: 978-1-937988-63-0

ISBN eBook: 978-1-937988-62-3

ISBN Hardcover: 978-1-937988-64-7

Hunter's Moon Publishing

https://HuntersMoonPublishing.com

Hunter's Moon Publishing - Connie Ragen Green

P.O. Box 3295

Santa Barbara, CA 93130-3295

Connect with Connie Ragen Green at ConnieRagenGreen.com

Connie Ragen Green's Titles

- *In Pursuit of Healthy-Ness: How I Reinvented My Life with Intermittent Fasting*

- *Speakers! The Quick Public Speaking to Business Method™ - Turning Your Talk into an Ongoing Revenue Stream*

- *The Road Trip: An Entrepreneur's Journey of Self-Discovery*

- *Authors! The Quick Book to Business Method™ - Turning Your Book into an Ongoing Revenue Stream*

- *Local Business Marketing: Making the Phone Ring for Businesses Everywhere*

- *Doing What It Takes: The Online Entrepreneur's Playbook*

- *Kids and Money – Teaching Financial Responsibility and Values to Children*

- *Rethinking the Work Ethic: Embrace the Struggle and Exceed Your Own Potential*

- *The Transformational Entrepreneur: Creating a Life of Dedication and Service*

- *Book. Blog. Broadcast. The Trifecta of Entrepreneurial Success*

- *Write. Publish. Prosper. How to Write Prolifically, Publish Globally, and Prosper Eternally*

- *Living the Internet Lifestyle: Quit Your Job, Become an Entrepreneur, and Live Your Ideal Life*

- *The Inner Game of Internet Marketing – with Geoff Hoff*

- *The Weekend Marketer: Say Goodbye to the '9 to 5', Build an Online Business, and Live the Life You Love*

- *Time Management Strategies for Entrepreneurs: How to Manage Your Time to Increase Your Bottom Line – with Geoff Hoff*

- *Huge Profits with a Tiny List: 50 Ways to Use Relationship Marketing to Increase Your Bottom Line*

- *Essays at the Intersection of Hope and Synchronicity*

... and too many more to mention!

Dedication

My life's journey, so far has been one of wonder, anticipation, and fulfillment. My expectations continue to rise and my connections with people all over the world who seek a similar path grow daily.

Achieving my goal of inspiring those I meet to strive to create and live the life they want and deserve is my life's work and legacy.

My overall dedication of this book is to everyone who has ever looked in the mirror and told themselves that they know there is a better life awaiting them, and that they are willing to seek out the people who can help them to make their dreams a reality.

From my own experiences and life lessons that are ongoing, I will tell you there is definitely something more wonderful waiting for you to embrace it, and it all begins with living a self-directed life.

My personal dedication is to Sanna, a very special person who came into my life in the year 2000. We met in person a year later, and soon I could not imagine my life without her and her children. We are extended family by choice, and although she is two decades younger than I am, Sanna continues to teach and nurture and guide me towards keeping all of my projects and adventures on track and living my best life. Living on opposite sides of the pond can sometimes be a challenge, but perhaps this part of our intricate and loving relationship makes it even more precious and sacred to me.

Keep an open mind and welcoming heart as you work your way through what I have created for you here. And know that everything is possible when you shift your mindset and outlook on the path that lies ahead.

Forewords

A Chance Encounter

Connie and I met on an airplane. Actually, it was at the airport lounge before the flight. No, that's not right. I first made Connie's acquaintance while we were both going through security at LAX.

That is exactly the moment where my gaze met hers and for a brief moment the world stood still. Allow me to explain...

I am a corporate trainer in the areas of sales, negotiation, and advertising. This means that I am brought in to help corporations improve their bottom line by serving their clients and customers in a mutually beneficial way, and in a manner that naturally increases revenue. This is unique work that I am well suited to, and something that keeps me in high demand.

This work takes me all over the world and I breathe my work 24/7, by choice. I was widowed in 2001. My son is almost thirty and newly married. My stepson is two years older and an attorney. They both live in Austin, Texas and I see them at least once each month for several days. Other than that, my life is my work and for that I am grateful.

On the late fall day when my path crossed with Connie's, I was on my way to Helsinki to meet with clients at Nokia. They are a global telecommunications, information technology, and consumer electronics corporation based in Espoo, Finland.

I had absentmindedly left my bag containing my headphones and some keys on the conveyor belt after going through security. Connie saw me dashing away, grabbed the bag and practically jumped in front of me to force me to stop.

Without saying a word, she rearranged her bags and held mine up in the air. She was smiling, and I was immediately put at ease. A fellow traveler, apparently not as weary as me was my angel.

"Thank you" was all I could get out. It was noisy and crowded in the area where the Global Entry members merged with the rest of the crowd in order to move closer to the gates.

"Yes, of course." She answered is a gentle way and our fingers brushed when I took the bag from her hand.

That could have been the end of our chance encounter. It wasn't. Ten minutes later she was beside me in the Delta Lounge. She motioned to a small table overlooking the lower level. It was a corner table with two chairs, and I could see that she'd already placed her items on one side.

I nodded back at her and made my way through the others who were also taking a break and enjoying some snacks.

We quickly discovered that we would not only be on the same flights – first to Amsterdam, and then after a two hour layover on to Helsinki – but that we had much in common as well.

For the next hour we exchanged life stories. She had lost her first husband and understood how that can feel. The emptiness from such an abrupt loss is something that doesn't ever leave you completely. We had also both helped raise stepchildren that we love as our own.

Then, there is the entrepreneur thing. Most of my acquaintances are either employees or contact workers. The few that define themselves as entrepreneurs probably aren't really, but we never go that level of introspection with our friendships.

I have to say that it was refreshing to meet someone who was born to be an entrepreneur, yet didn't discover her calling until the age of fifty.

As for me, I have never held a job. Even in high school, I started businesses in order to make money and help out my parents. I serviced swimming pools, delivered (and eventually notarized) legal documents, and hauled trash to the dump. Working for someone else felt too limiting and confining, and would not have fit into my busy schedule.

We shared ideas on that day, along with the stories, and then we laughed as we spontaneously and simultaneously pulled pens and small notebooks out to make some notes. Great minds thinking alike, we exclaimed.

Next, it was the writing thing. I had always wanted to write, but didn't. Connie too!

I finally decided to write and found it to be the most difficult activity in the world. Connie too.

While I was still in college, I gave up the idea of writing at a more serious level and with the intention of publishing books and other writing. Not Connie.

This is where our paths diverge. I have to admit that it wasn't until we had left the lounge, boarded the first leg of our flight, realized we had aisle seats across from one another, and resumed our conversation that I had something of an epiphany. It shook me to my very core and made emotions raise up inside of me that I had not been at all familiar with during my life.

What was I feeling? Regret. I was suddenly and very powerfully regretful that I had not made much effort with my writing. I had shied away from the hard work, the discipline, the rejection, and everything else that comes along with going after your dreams.

Connie, instead, had wrestled her dream into submission. She told me about the two-hundred-fifty word articles she struggled to write, the embarrassment she felt as a former teacher, around her writing, and the times she thought her writing would never improve, until she thought back to what she had told her students years earlier.

She shared that the majority of her students were not native English speakers. She quickly discovered that writing would be the most challenging part of their academic life. Then she gave them advice that made a difference to those who took it to heart…

Connie told them they needed to write every single day: weekends, holidays, vacations. If they did this, even a few sentences every day, their writing would improve. She promised them this, and it happened.

Then, in 2006 she told me that it was then when the rubber hit the road. She said she was ready to take her own advice, finally, after twenty years of giving it to children from all over the world.

The secret to this working for her was in what she noticed with her students. They were too close to their own writing to see the changes and improvements that slowly accrued. The same was true for her. It was only when a close friend read one of her blog posts several months after she began and called her on the phone. In that moment, she cried with joy because she could finally see it, through the eyes of her friend.

She was so encouraged on that day that she committed to becoming a published author, and she has, many times over.

When I wrote earlier that the world stood still the first time I looked into Connie's eyes, I did not know at that moment how to unpack that feeling. It wasn't love at first sight or a premonition of something to come.

Instead, it was a peaceful feeling that washed over me. I knew that some part of my life was finally going to come together after so many years of almost always feeling that something was missing. It was kind of like thinking you might have left the lights on or didn't make a call before you left the house.

By the time we landed in Helsinki, almost fifteen hours after we had first met, a part of my life, the missing piece, was finally in place. I was a writer, and I now spend time every single day writing something, anything, even a few sentences, just like Connie used to instruct her students to do. Now I'm one of them.

Lance Morgan

March 25, 2023

Sante Fe, New Mexico

One in a Million

I have been to more places throughout the world with Connie Ragen Green than with anyone else in my life. We are close friends in the truest sense of that word. We have never been romantically involved, yet we are soulmates.

My name is Eugene Norris and I grew up in Miami, Florida with my parents and three siblings. Connie and her mother moved in next door to us the summer I turned ten and she was twelve.

Our friendship started as a fortuitous one, but not random by any means. I am positive that she would have much rather befriended a girl her age who would also be going to junior high in September. Or, it would have been more likely that she would have spent time with my older brother, one of the popular kids already in junior high and going into the 9th grade that fall.

But it was me she talked to each day after school and me she wanted to ride bikes with to learn about her new neighborhood.

Connie wasn't shy, but she didn't talk to most people on our street, unless they spoke to her first. Then she would open up and that's how I learned about how her and her mom came to live next door to me and my family.

They had been in California since Connie was born. They fell on hard times, her parents divorced, and her father remarried and started a new family.

Her mom thought it would be easier for them in Miami for a number of reasons. They rode the train from Los Angeles to downtown Miami and arrived in the middle of the night.

A favorite story Connie shares, and she has many stories, is one related to this cross-country train ride. They were just outside of Baton

Rouge, Louisiana and the train slowed to a stop. It was the middle of the night and the conductor came through the cars and told everyone to gather their belongings and get off the train.

In a hilariously dramatic manner, Connie reenacts that morning and does an imitation of the conductor walking up and down the aisles and saying, "You've arrived! Prepare to disembark."

It turned out they had to make some type of minor repairs and that was why they were put out in the middle of nowhere in the wee hours of the morning. Someone started a fire in a metal trash container, and everyone gathered around to warm themselves until they were allowed back on the train several hours later.

Connie would tell people that her father had promised to come and visit, but she said she thought she wouldn't ever see him again. It was sad to hear her say that. I think each time she did a part of her died a little bit and another part came to life, if that makes any sense.

My life wasn't great either, with an alcoholic father and a mother who I thought would rather be anywhere else than home with four kids.

Our bikes were our ticket to freedom. After school, we met up at the park down the street and took off on adventures we never shared with anyone else. Saturday mornings were the most fun, with a full day in front of us and no one checking on where we were.

One weekend we rode all the way to Fort Lauderdale. That was about twenty-five miles north of Miami and we didn't even know anyone there or have a particular destination in mind. Within an hour we were so hot and sweaty we had to stop and rest. When some people walked by and asked us where we were headed, we answered "Florida" and laughed until our sides ached.

A few years later Connie and her mother moved to another part of Miami and we lost track of each other. Then someone told me she had gotten married and lived in an apartment near the big library and I took the bus to find her.

When I did find her apartment building, I didn't recognize her after not seeing her for almost two years. She was sitting on the front stoop of the building and had a toddler on each side of her. I knew they weren't hers, but seeing her with them made me know that she was still my friend.

She said it would be okay if I came to visit when I had time. I did go a few times and her husband was always nice to me. He was much older so I know he thought of me as a boy. But perhaps that's why he didn't mind me coming to visit and spending some time with Connie and his little kids.

Then they moved up to Gainesville so Connie could go to the college there. I figured we wouldn't see each other ever again, but I was wrong.

One day she called me out of the blue. She said everything was fine, but that she missed me. She asked me if I'd heard about the new Disneyland opening up. Yes, I had heard about it, everyone had.

We made a plan to meet there the following weekend. I would take the bus to Orlando and she would drive down from Gainesville to pick me up.

It was so much fun and I was sad when it was over. But that was when I finally knew we were friends for life and that Connie had no plans to ever throw that away.

That weekend was fifty years ago. Since then, Connie and I have lived our lives on separate coasts with very different experiences.

Time and technology have made the distance shorter and our friendship stronger. It has also taught us that we have more in common after all this time than we could have ever imagined.

We both love animals and gardening and traveling and helping others. We each have a sadness within us that has developed into a resilience more strong and powerful than the tallest building made of steel.

At times, we are almost like twins who sense when the other is in need. And then there are the times when it's almost like we are strangers with no reason to stay in touch.

One thing I know for certain is that we are each better people because we know each other. I read everything she writes and she listens to every story I need to share.

I have a photo of us I carry with me wherever I go. It's from 1992 when Connie came back to live in Miami for a short time. We're at the beach with a couple of people we knew from school. The sun is in our eyes and the waves behind us have a sparkle to them.

A week after that photo was taken, Hurricane Andrew destroyed the house where she was living and it would be three days before I knew she had survived. She came to stay with me after that, and less than a month later she found out she had breast cancer. I did a lot of crying and praying during that time. Maybe she knew, but maybe she's finding out about it here for the first time.

Connie is one in a million, and since you are reading this book perhaps you already know that.

Eugene Norris

March 21, 2023

Miami, Florida

Preface

Twice in my life I've arrived at a crossroads of sorts. One time it was around my health, and the other around my work and financial situation. I'll share a bit of each of these pivotal moments with you here…

I was looking directly at my computer screen, yet I couldn't, or didn't want to believe what I was reading. It was the results of my latest bloodwork and my numbers were off the charts.

I'd been here before. It was three years previous to this day, back in December of 2019. At my annual physical, the new doctor had shown me the results of my most recent blood work; my numbers were all headed in the wrong direction and he told me that at this rate I would no longer be prediabetic.

No, this time he was predicting that I would be a full-on diabetic within the next 90 days and he was also recommending several medications, in addition to test kits, measuring devices, and a consultation from someone who helped patients to monitor their diabetes so it did not escalate into even more serious illnesses and conditions.

He opened the exam room door and asked an assistant to join us. With a flurry of activity, they updated my chart on the screen and in my folder, a call was made to the lab and to the pharmacy, and my life changed before my eyes and in a way I did not want to acknowledge.

I left the medical office on that day wondering where I had gone wrong; didn't I know this could happen if I neglected to eat and exercise according to what had been working for the past three years? The world had fast-forwarded to 2023 in a blur, yet I had managed to drift off course and was now stranded on an island all alone.

As if this current health predicament were not enough, I was beginning to question what I was doing each day and the direction I was heading with my online business.

Perhaps I had grown weary of helping others to achieve a six-figure annual income as authors, marketers, and online entrepreneurs, or longed for more intense projects to be involved with, but for whatever reason I had lost some of the excitement I had experienced with working with people in this way since 2006.

Many of those I'd mentored had achieved great success, yet there were also others who had not ascended the plateau to replacing, or at least supplementing their income to be able to live what I describe as a "lifestyle by design" that comes with time and financial freedom.

There were plenty of circumstances unfolding in the world where I could place blame. The pandemic. The economy. The threat of nuclear war. You only had to go as far as the local supermarket to see the continuing supply chain issues. People all around the world were suffering in ways reminiscent of the Great Depression and World War II. While I hadn't been alive during those events, my reading and discussions with others opened my eyes to what could be on the horizon.

As I turned off my computer so as not have to gaze at the alarming A1C and other numbers in my health chart, I went for a walk to think about my life in a way I hadn't before, and to assess my best options for moving forward.

It was January of 2023 and I was ready to once again change my life. But instead of doing this in the way I had in years past, I knew that this time I had more to gain by creating a plan designed to allow me to reach for goals and dreams I had long left behind, in order to not online improve my outlook on life in general, but to, more specifically, save my life in a way that would make everything I'd done in the past look like child's play. In short, I was ready to live a self-directed life.

In this book, I am taking you along on my journey, not back to where I was previously at any point along the way where I believed I had finally arrived at my destination; no, I'm taking you on the journey I had an inkling of but did not have the confidence to pursue in years past. Come aboard, buckle in, hang on tight, and let's explore this parallel universe together, shall we?

Contents

Introduction

"For want of a nail the shoe was lost, for want of a shoe the horse was lost; and for want of a horse the rider was lost; being overtaken and slain by the enemy, all for want of care about a horse-shoe nail."

~ Benjamin Franklin, The Way to Wealth... 1758

If you're new to this concept of self-direction, or skeptical about the results you'll be able to achieve with what I'm sharing with you here, know that you are not alone.

In fact, most of the people I know personally, both in my day-to-day life and within the online community have doubts. They aren't so sure that they can make such a radical shift in their thinking, belief system, and actions by using a series of simple strategies and interactions in order to get from where they are right now to closer to where they want to be in all areas of their life. These areas include personal relationships, health and wellness, prosperity and finances, and inner peace.

It is my sincere hope that you are motivated and inspired by what I am sharing with you here. The butterfly effect allows us all to pay it forward with every breath and step we take, impacting future generations in ways we cannot possibly fathom in the present moment.

The "butterfly effect" is the idea that small things can have non-linear impacts on a complex system. The concept is imagined with a butterfly flapping its wings in one part of the world and causing a typhoon in a distant location.

Of course, a single act like the butterfly flapping its wings cannot cause a typhoon. Small events can, however, serve as catalysts that act on starting conditions.

May you be the butterfly that graces the gardens of all those you encounter as you set about to live a self-directed life.

Section One

What Does It Mean to Be Self-Directed?

"Perhaps the most exciting realization in the world is finally understanding that living the life of your dreams is entirely up to you. It's also about the scariest."

~ Mike Dooley

What does it mean to be "self-directed" and to live a self-directed life? Definitions include ones around pursuing an activity under one's own control, as well as a person showing initiative and the ability to organize oneself and one's goals.

Going deeper within and beyond these dictionary listings, you'll find discussions around "self-directed learning," "self-directed personality," and "self-directed thinking" to mention just a few.

Also, I will add here that I am not suggesting you go through life alone, or without a belief in God, the Universe, or a higher power that meets your needs and expectations, while also being on par with your core values and beliefs.

If anything, our faith enforces the belief system that protects and guides us in each moment to achieve our full potential.

A person who is self-directed will recognize that their attitudes, behaviors, and problems reflect their own choices.

According to studies conducted by Baker & Brown in 1984 and Sternberg in 1986, self-directed thinking is the control factor in metacognition, a major component of intelligence dealing with the knowledge and awareness of individual thought. It is metacognition that enables students of any age and setting to recognize opportunities for learning, and multiplies the effects of instruction.

Self-directed learning can be as diverse as simply discovering new information and thinking critically about it, actively participating, and also contributing to a learning community, or designing your own learning path and selecting resources, guides and information.

I struggled for two decades to be able to implement a model of at least a partial degree of self-directed learning in my classrooms, but the administration could not understand why this model would be beneficial to my students.

Throughout this book, I will share how you can strive to become more self-directed in every aspect of your life, and how this will make a difference in a way that nothing else I have ever encountered has ever made for me, and for those close to me, both personally and professionally.

Before we can make any significant changes to our life, we must first step forward and raise our hand to accept the precept that although none of us knows it all, we all know enough to embrace change when it makes sense, and especially when the path we are on is no longer working in our favor and our basic needs are not being served in the way they could be, if only we were brave enough to see and be this change.

Chapter One

Embracing the Self-Directed Path

"There is always light, if only we're brave enough to see it. If only we're brave enough to be it."

~ Amanda Gorman

Change is never easy. My first name, Connie, comes from the Latin and means "constant; never changing." For decades, I wore this label proudly and it served as an excuse for my shortcomings.

I'll speak to this limiting belief in a chapter near the very end of this book in much greater detail, as it has had a profound effect on the trajectory of my life.

I didn't want to budge when it came to my beliefs about almost everything. This included the clothes I wore, the people I spent time with, the make and model of the cars I drove, the universities I attended, the career path I took, the foods I consumed, and the relationships I entertained.

Back then, no part of my life was motivated or inspired by the people around me, the books I read, or the experiences I was engaged in each day. Instead, my outlook on life became one that could be boiled down to a few sentences, and these days would be turned into a meme.

I believed wholeheartedly that *other people* could do the things I could not. These things included being a part of a healthy, happy, and loving relationship, having a career that brought both challenge and satisfaction, maintaining excellent health and wellness, and enjoying financial independence as a result of understanding finance, investments, and economics.

It wasn't that everyone around me was enjoying this lifestyle I was craving, and that I was the only one who was left out. I knew people that appeared, at least from my limited and somewhat biased perspective, to have command of one or two of these areas. Yet, there was always one piece of their puzzle that didn't quite fit.

During my twenties, I began to have the belief that it wasn't possible to have everything in your life go well at all times. Couples I knew would have some type of issue that could not be resolved and choose to divorce. A close friend or family member would be diagnosed with cancer, and that sometimes ended their life abruptly. Someone would be forced to file bankruptcy because of a seemingly unavoidable chain of events. A friend would lose their job and return to college to be able to start over in a new career.

There were no promises or guarantees that the relationships, health, finances, and career you had at some point would continue into the distant future. I was feeling like I was stranded alone on an island, and that theme would be a recurring one for the next three decades.

If you're feeling like this right now, or have entertained similar thoughts and beliefs in the past, then you're in the right place.

The human condition does not have to be one of loneliness, struggle, and disappointment. You deserve to wake up each day knowing that you have control over the experiences you have chosen to encounter, and that you are entitled and expected to have great joy and success throughout each day. It's your birthright and is waiting for you, right around the corner. Knowing which corner to turn on is the key, and I'll be sharing the exact coordinated with you as you continue to read what I am sharing with you here.

Where Are You Right Now?

As I shared in the Preface, I was once again facing a health crisis I thought I had diverted forever, at the beginning of 2023. I had gone from spending two and a half years easily maintaining my intermittent fasting practice, dropping more than a hundred twenty pounds (55 kilos) and feeling and looking better than I had in more than two decades, to inching closer to the lowest point I had ever experienced in regards to my health, ready to fall off the cliff and into the abyss, in just a matter of eight months or so.

This downward spiral had begun sometime in the summer of 2022, though I could not put my finger on exactly what triggered this change in my thinking and behavior. My excellent habits and actions had somehow slipped away, and only I was to blame for this unexpected shift.

Almost simultaneously, I began to doubt myself in other areas of my life. These included my relationships with family, friends, colleagues, and business associates, as well as with my online business and my writing.

I'll be sharing my progress with you here, all of it based upon my thoughts, feelings, beliefs, and actions that shape everything I, and everyone else engages in throughout each day.

Accountability As a Habit

As a measure of self-accountability — the most reliable and valuable kind, in my opinion - I want you to keep a journal, digital or physical while you are going through this book. By tracking your progress, you'll be in a better position to begin and to continue to make significant changes to your own life and experiences.

And, if journaling has not been an effective strategy for you in years past, I will recommend that you begin each new day of journaling by spending some time reading through what you wrote previously, and then copying those words into your journal as a copywork practice. Yes, I'll go into greater details about the power and benefits of copywork later on as well.

What are the specific areas where you want and need to make some changes? While many people believe that it's best if you only focus on one area of your life at a time, I recommend more of a wholistic approach to making broad, sweeping changes to as many areas as you want to right now.

Your journal is just for you to write in and refer to, so be completely honest with yourself. It wasn't easy for me to write down that I weighed three hundred two pounds when I began my intermittent fasting journey in the spring of 2020, but it sure felt good to later know that I'd had a more than hundred-pound weight loss because of the work I was willing to do.

When I started my online business in 2006, I was just a few months away from losing my home and everything I had worked for over the past two decades, but it sure made me feel proud of myself when I surpassed my previous income and continued to grow my savings less than two years later.

Self-accountability as a habit will lead you closer to living the self-directed life I am writing about within these pages.

Goal Setting and Achieving

With great effort comes great rewards, and you deserve everything you will build and grow and achieve in your life.

I will add something here about goals and goal setting. You may already know that writing down your goal is the best way to actually achieve it. If you know this and aren't doing it with everything you want in your life, ask yourself why not.

I have been a part of a goal setting and achieving program since 2005. It was created by my first mentor, Raymond Aaron, and without him and this program I'm not sure where I would be and what my life might be like right now.

Each month, we fill out a form with the areas we are going to work on in our life. These include:

- Mess: This could be a pile of papers on the floor of our office, or a situation that arose with a friend, or any of a number of other messes that have become evident to us.

- Acknowledgement: It's important to acknowledge the people who are making a difference in our life. The first time I did this I called my closest friend and told her how much her friendship had meant to me over the years.

  I thanked her for helping me become a real estate appraiser back in 1989, and for taking me shopping when I had been asked to speak at a marketing conference for the first time in 2007. She broke in part way and said, "Oh, no. You don't have cancer again, do you Connie?" We can laugh about that conversation now, but at the time I had never spoken to the people in my life in this heartfelt manner.

- Increase In Wealth: Each month I look for a new income stream or source of income, or a way to increase something I'm already involved with in my business. The result has been a steady increase in income each month over the years, and this includes the time during the 2008 Recession, as well as the Pandemic that began in 2020.

- New: It's so easy to do the same 'ol thing all the time. I was definitely in a rut when I began this goal setting program and I wasn't sure what the best use of my time would be. I've had fun with this one, from learning how to line dance to playing pickleball to creating an oil painting!

- Learn: While I was a classroom teacher, I wanted to impress upon my students the idea that we are all lifelong learners. I was always taking a class or two on Saturdays or an evening during the week.

⚘ Yourself: Thinking back, I do not believe I had ever heard about self-care before starting this program. When Raymond described how he and his wife pampered themselves, I was judgmental in my belief that it was something only rich people would do. It didn't take long for me to come to the realization that perhaps they were rich *because* of how they took care of themselves.

Another part of my goal setting and achieving practice is to decide how much time and effort I will put into each of these areas in my life. I choose if I will do the minimum, hit a specific target, or go above and beyond and achieve an outrageous goal in that area.

For example, I may decide to only pick up all the papers on the floor in my office (minimum), pick everything up and go through each item to throw away and file them (target), or get a filing cabinet and sort and file each item for easy retrieval in the future (outrageous). I enjoy seeing my progress in each area in real time each month, and continue to challenge myself to make incremental improvements.

I should add that Raymond's goal setting and achieving program is much more detailed and comprehensive than I'm able to share with you here. But I'm sure you get the idea that this is an important part of embracing a life where self-direction is your road map and guidance system.

The Journey is a Continuous One

First, I'm going to drop some semantics and clarification into what I'm sharing with you here. It's around the words continuous and continual. 'Continuous' refers to something that happens without ever ceasing or being interrupted, while 'continual' refers to something that recurs frequently or regularly.

If your thoughts and actions are continual, then you are in a constant state of disruption and flux while you take the time and energy to get back on track each time. Instead, strive for a continuous process of learning and growing in every waking moment of your days.

My life's journey continues to be a work in progress and I am in the process of becoming the person I truly want to be. This thinking came to me while I was working as a classroom teacher in the inner city of Los Angeles from 1986 until 2006.

My students were stuck in beliefs around a precept that the person they were on any specific day was the one they would be forever. When I discovered this, I was determined to help them shift their thinking. It turned out I needed to do the same thing, so this became a class project.

I began by asking them to think about how they physically appeared at that moment. Then, I had them visualize how they had looked in the past, perhaps in a school picture or at a family gathering.

Their assignment was to find photographs at home, and to bring one or two to school to share with our class. Of course, the older the photo the greater the difference in their appearance. I would do this right along with them. I loved sharing what I looked like when I was about their age, and also how I looked as a younger adult.

We would all laugh hysterically for a few minutes, and then I commenced to begin the discussion, including an in-depth question and answer exercise.

- ☀ Were they surprised at what I looked like earlier in my life?

- ☀ Could they recognize me from a photo taken so long ago? How? What were the most obvious visual clues?

- ☀ What thoughts came into their minds when they looked at older photos of themselves and their classmates? How did their feelings and emotions play into this?

- ☀ Did they understand that all of us continue to change our physical appearance over time?

☀ Could they relate physical appearance to other areas of their lives, such as interests, athletic and academic performance, and attitudes and ideas about their future?

Yes, we went deep with this, and everyone, including me benefitted immensely from our discussions.

Why Self-Direction Finally Made Sense for Me

In 2005 I had reached a crossroads in my life. I thought of myself as being happy and positive, yet it was mostly a feeling of contentment and of settling for a life that wasn't quite meeting my expectations. That's when I began telling myself stories.

The dominant theme in my stories was that I was doing as well as could be expected, for someone like me. Other people were capable of achieving more, and with good reason; they were smarter, came from better families, were better connected, had better social skills, and had been used to a very different life than I had experienced.

The truth is, we all believe our life experiences and stories are unique, but they aren't. Humans around the world have much more in common than we like to believe. I have now traveled extensively in countries where I used to be amazed at the similarities of the people and with what we shared in common.

I'm going to share a story with you here, and it is one I believe will make a difference and resonate with you as you continue reading this book…

It was a summer evening during 1994, and the traffic was light for a Saturday night, I thought. My gaze drifted from the street back to the other person seated at my table. She sat directly across from me, looking me up and down before she spoke.

I was in Stockholm, and it was my first trip to Europe. I so wanted to make a good impression with this woman.

Karl, the man I had come to Europe to see, had introduced her to me an hour earlier as Margaret, his school mate from long ago. I smiled, making sure to not do it too broadly, but not to hold back either. The "just right" smile was on my lips as I waited for her to speak.

"Hmm... Never been to Europe until now." It was more of a judgmental statement than a question, as I had offered up this fact to the group just minutes earlier. I was thirty-nine years old at this time, and hoped she wouldn't want too detailed an explanation of my travel experience.

"No, I didn't come because I wasn't sure where to go or what to see. I wasn't really a student of history when I was younger and I don't – didn't know anyone who lived here until several months ago."

It was awkward and clumsy, but it was honest. I was in Europe now, and that seemed to be the most important part of what she was implying.

"And now you're here, on the Continent. What do you do in America? Have you a job?" Margaret wanted to figure me out, and now I was anxious and willing to oblige.

"Yes, I'm a teacher. I teach elementary school." She tilted her head to one side and I realized she needed more details.

"My students, this year anyway, are in the 6th grade. That makes them eleven and twelve, except for Isaih; he came from Mexico and had never been in school before. He's thirteen and we're hoping he can learn enough English and reading skills to go to Middle School in the fall."

I'd said too much, and knew I was blathering on, and Margaret looked confused or disinterested, I couldn't tell which. But I continued.

"Isaih is a Hebrew name that means 'God is salvation' in Hebrew. People were calling him Isaac or Isaiah, but I thought it might even be a misspelling of the name Ismael. That name – Ismael – is popular, especially with the Spanish and Portuguese versions. It means 'God will hear' and this was Abraham's sons' name in the Old Testament. And in the Old Testament, that name spelled 'Isaiah' is one of the most important major prophets and the author of the Book of Isaiah."

She was silent. I thought she looked down at her watch and I imagined she was thinking up a story so she could leave the restaurant. Anything, to not have to listen to me drone on and on any longer.

We were distracted by dishes clanging together at a table two over from ours. Margaret turned to look back at me and I seized the moment.

"I actually mispronounced his name – Isaih's – when he was first in my class. He told me it was okay but I told him it wasn't okay with me and shouldn't be with him. So, he taught me how to pronounce it – his name – and after I practiced, I got it right and now it's in my brain."

"Evidently." She raised her eyebrows at me, then got the attention of a waitress and signaled with an extended right index finger that she needed more coffee.

"It was also the name of the person who narrates the Herman Melville book, you know, Moby Dick."

Would I ever shut up? Why was I so nervous? I needed to ask her something about herself.

"Did you always want to be a journalist? What types of stories do you write? Did you go to college to learn this style of writing?"

Boom, boom, boom, my questions flew at her like basketballs and landed solidly in her face. The ball was in her court and I gave her time to lob it back.

"Yes, all types, and no, I'm self-taught, for the most part. Writing is my life."

We sat in silence for a few moments, allowing the chatter of other patrons to wash over us gently, as a reminder to me that you can learn much about a person simply by sitting across from them. I was in awe of her now, someone who considered writing to be such an important part of her life, in a way I had dreamed of but hadn't taken action on in my own life.

Margaret smiled. Then, she crossed her arms and sat back in her chair for a minute before speaking again.

"Have you anything besides the teaching? How else do you spend your time?"

"I'm a real estate broker. And I am also a residential property appraiser." I decided not to share the details unless she asked. I bit my tongue until I tasted blood to keep myself from speaking again until she did.

"Really. Why would you do both? There must be a story there and I'd like to hear it."

And so, she would. I went on for what seemed like an hour, sharing the details of why I had gone into real estate in my early twenties, why I became a teacher, and why I'd decided not to give up real estate after earning my teaching credential and getting a job in the classroom.

And then I shared what I believed would be the most interesting part of all to her and might even give me some credibility: How and why I was able to become a Certified Residential Property Appraiser in the State of California, during the first year this type of national certification became available and required in the United States.

Her face lit up, and each time it did it encouraged me to provide more details. I leaned in and went back in time to when I was a child to make my story more interesting and complete.

I had grown up very poor, raised by a single mother, and we had always wanted to live in a house of our own. When I was twelve, I read an ad in the Sunday newspaper about some land for sale near a place called Orlando. We were living in Miami at the time and it was a couple of hundred miles north of us.

I saved up the money I was earning from mowing lawns and babysitting and other odd jobs. Then, I bought a money order at the post office and mailed it to them for the down payment and first payment of ten dollars each, so twenty bucks in all.

One day about a month later, there was a knock at the door and a man asked for me. My mother told him he had the wrong address until I jumped up from doing my homework in front of the television and I announced that he was looking for me. I had neglected to mention to her that I was now a property owner, even if it was raw land and we weren't close enough to actually see it or walk on it.

The three of us sat at our kitchen table and my mother signed her name to make it all legal. Then the man asked us if we'd like to fly up for the weekend and visit the property. Neither my mother nor I had never flown, but we mustered up the courage to say yes, we would come.

"What happened to that piece of property?" She was leaning in and maintaining eye contact, a sign, at least to me that she was more interested in the end of this story than in the part in the middle that I so wanted to tell her about. I looked swiftly to my left and then to the right, and then looked at her directly in the eyes to emphasize that was I was about to say was not common knowledge to most people who had met me.

"I paid it off while I was in college and a few years later sold it to a man I met who was looking for investments. The land had appreciated significantly after they opened Disney World in that area of Florida in '71, so I used the money as a down payment on a house in California.

"You're a clever girl."

And there it was. Margaret had come to the conclusion that I was someone worth her time. That hadn't been so difficult, after all. Perhaps I was more interesting than I gave myself credit for being, and maybe I was even smarter than I thought. But none of that mattered. The only thing that was important was that Karl would hear from her that I was a "keeper," however they described that in the Swedish culture. I knew he wanted to marry me and having his friends from childhood get to know me was his way of vetting me before he got too involved.

I excused myself to the ladies' room and took my time about it. I needed to think this through and work it out in my mind. It will be okay, I kept telling myself, but I was crying by the time I locked the water closet door behind me.

Clever. I thought of monkeys as being clever, but only because they were smart when it came to getting what they wanted. Was it a compliment? I'd taken it that way and thought I should leave it alone. Clever Connie. Connie the clever little monkey. I washed my hands, threw cold water over my face, and attempted to shake it off.

Upon returning to the cafe floor and spotting our table several minutes later, I saw that Karl and another man had joined Margaret. They were laughing and reminiscing about their school days. Karl jumped up to embrace me and kissed me on the cheek. I knew he could tell that I'd been crying. His gentle gaze into my eyes put me at ease and we all sat down.

Dinner was served and I had the Swedish meatballs. They were served with the creamed mashed potatoes I loved, instead of the more traditional salty noodles and I silently congratulated myself for noticing that on the menu. As we ate and talked and laughed, my smile was broader than usual and totally inappropriate. Clever indeed.

Over the next few months, I came to define the term clever in a way that honored Margaret's intention and my opinion of my own self-worth. A person is clever when they excel at problem solving and are able to achieve even the loftiest of goals without the benefit of advantages others may enjoy. To be clever is to be able to create a lifestyle by design and on your terms.

Yet, it would be another decade before I truly took her words to heart and began to think more highly of myself. The self-directed life opens your mind to what's possible, and you'll discover that much of it has been there all along.

Chapter Two

Stepping Outside the Box

"The only way to make sense out of change is to plunge into it, move with it, and join the dance."

— Alan Watts

The self-directed life will require you to take a leap of faith while blindfolded. Lest those words sound too scary and perhaps esoteric and abstract as you read them aloud, let me share that I have found the human life experience to be one of multiple twists and turns.

Life is messy at times, and on some days you will wish for a magic wand to wave over your situations to make everything turn out the way you want, and right now.

Remaining within the confines of your comfort zone got you to where you are right now. That's important to remember, because we can only start from where we are, acknowledge that we made great strides in our progress, and are now ready to get out of our own way in order to move forward.

I believe we must have no regrets, and only joy and hope that it is the exact time for us to move boldly forward.

No One Was Betting I'd Do What It Takes to Succeed

On a recent winter evening I was with friends at an event for the Santa Barbara Film Festival that honored the directors of the films "Tár" and "The Banshees of Inisherin" as well as the lesser-known actors in each of these films, who overcame great odds to achieve their success. My friends have known me for over thirty years, and at one point one of them nudged me and said,

"Who would have expected us to be invited to something like this?" I nodded in agreement. This made me think about the expectations people in our lives have for us, and how little was expected of me when I was younger.

No one in my earlier life was betting on me to succeed. My mother and I had been homeless twice while I was in elementary school; I began earning money babysitting and mowing lawns when I was eleven; and at fourteen I was a hostess at the local pancake house and begged the manager to let me be a waitress on the weekends to earn tips. These were the first steps out of poverty for my mother and I, but I couldn't see a future.

Several years later I would get married. I was not yet eighteen and my mother reluctantly gave her permission. Bob was ten years older and had returned from serving two years in Vietnam just months earlier. His life had fallen apart when his wife announced she wanted a divorce and did not want to help raise their two toddlers.

When I met him, his parents had already taken custody and were moving forward with adoption. He and I had a loving relationship based on mutual respect and a desire to make a better life for ourselves and for the children.

I understand now what people thought of me entering into a marriage with an older man at my young age. They were honestly concerned for my wellbeing and future and did not want me to regret later on what I was doing as a teenager with such limited life experience.

Looking back, I believe some of the people in my life at that time might have been afraid that I would end up divorced, trying to raise one or more children, and without a high school diploma, all by the time I was twenty-one.

Our marriage certainly wasn't perfect, but we were perfectly matched at that time. He insisted that I finish high school, which I did the following year through a program that would now be called a "continuation" school.

Then, he encouraged me to apply to college. I went first to a community college, then applied to and was accepted at the University of Florida in Gainesville. This is a city in the center of Florida, known for its dense forests and small-town atmosphere. It's the county seat of Alachua County and boasted a population of just under fifty thousand residents – including students – during the year we were there.

It wasn't easy for him to find work in Gainesville, but he was finally hired by a local company who assembled "Butler" buildings – these are pre-engineered metal buildings typically used for light industrial purposes.

The main office was located an hour south in Ocala and it was also closer for us to spend time with Bob's parents so we could be a part of the children's lives. When I was accepted to UCLA a year later, his parents agreed to let the kids go with us on a trial basis, and all of us packed up and moved to California, where I was from originally.

Bob died from leukemia a decade later, and those toddlers are the stepchildren I love so much and speak about often. They are also two of the small handful of people who are still living, with whom I have the longest continuity in my life.

I'm sharing these stories with you as a way to show that it doesn't matter if we come from humble beginnings; by setting expectations for ourselves and being willing to do what it takes, anything is possible.

Back to my story at the beginning of this chapter, of being at the event at the film festival: On the way out of the theater that night, Cate Blanchett told me that she loved my dress. Imagine that.

I used to be embarrassed to share personal details of my life, but I've come to believe that by laying ourselves bare we give others a better understanding of our hopes and dreams and willingness to help with anything we possibly can.

Taking a Stand and Finding Your Voice

At some point in everyone's life, they find a reason to step into the light. For some, this comes early with a significant childhood event. For others, it can take what seems like a lifetime. For me, I was approaching my fiftieth birthday and had an awakening of sorts.

How many times have you found yourself in a situation where you think about what you should have said after the fact? Maybe you said yes to something you really didn't want to do, or you allowed someone to belittle you without any kind of repercussion. This is a common problem, especially if you've been a people pleaser.

You may tend to keep all opinions to yourself because you don't like rocking the boat and constantly worry about making someone upset with you. This creates a huge inner struggle that causes much added anxiety, stress and other mental and physical issues. Like many people pleasers, you may find it difficult to speak up because you associate it with being mean, selfish or uncooperative. This simply isn't true. Finding your voice doesn't mean you have to lash out and be hurtful with your words. There are plenty of ways get your point across and stay true to yourself in a way that is effective and empathetic to the others involved.

When it comes to speaking up for what matters to you, it's important to do it in a way that is deliberate and intentional. First, get to the root of the problem and then decide what and why it's really bothering you. By doing this, you get a clear picture of what you want and don't want, and it makes it easier to convey that to the other person.

Choose your words wisely when confronting someone and make sure you don't come across as accusatory. Most people will put up the defenses quickly if they feel like they are being accused of something.

Stay neutral with your tone and be clear with your concerns. You could even offer a suggestion to help remedy the problem at hand. By doing it this way, you can still get your point across without causing hurt feelings or bad vibes between you and someone else.

We're only given so many hours each week to commit to the things that are important to us. If you consistently spend the majority of those precious moments bending over backwards for others, it will wear you down and leave you feeling resentful and unhappy.

For this reason, you need to get comfortable being a little selfish with how you spend your time and where you place your energy. But how do you begin to do that? First of all, take time to remember all the things that are important you and prioritize them at the top of your list.

Maybe you value down time with your family every weekend or you prefer "me time" to a night out with friends. When faced with a situation where you have to pick one or the other, keep in mind that choosing yourself over someone else doesn't make you a bad person. It simply means you're taking care of your mental and physical health so that you can give more to others in the long run. Reminding yourself that it's ok to be selfish once in a while will make it that much easier to speak up during those moments that call for your voice to be heard.

Add an unequivocal and forcefully emphatical "No!" to your vocabulary. If it's been a huge struggle for you to say the word no, out loud and in a way that gets the attention of the person you're intending it to land on, rest assured you're definitely not alone.

In fact, saying *no* may be one of the most difficult things in the world to do, especially for those that have people pleaser tendencies. You don't want to rock the boat or make anyone mad, so you simply go through life being a yes person.

The bad thing is, by not knowing how to say no enough, you are doing yourself and the world a disservice because you're sacrificing your wants, needs and opinions for the happiness of others. While this may seem like a noble thing to do to those reaping in the benefits of your "selflessness," all it does is cause you a huge inner struggle that ends in frustration and resentment.

Start small and visualize how a situation could have gone differently if you had of said no in the past. Then practice, practice, practice. Saying no doesn't mean you have to be rude and hurtful. You can be polite, but firm and still walk away knowing you did the right thing.

Timing is everything. Finding the right moment to voice your concerns is key when trying to find a solution that works for all parties involved. While you don't want to wait too long to discuss something that's on your mind, if you suddenly hit someone with a barrage of complaints out of the blue, it will most likely not end well.

Before you go and put someone on the spot, consider when they would be more apt to listen and engage in a healthy, two-sided chat. For example, instead of confronting a co-worker in the office about an issue you have, arrange a meeting during a time that works best for both of you or make it a lunch date so you can chat over neutral ground. Handling the situation in this way will serve both parties in the best way possible. It's much easier for the issue to be heard and resolved when the other person doesn't feel blindsided by your statements.

Sometimes, speaking up for yourself means not saying a single word. Silence is golden, and remaining silent when someone expects you to be upset can be one of the most powerful messages you can ever send. The fact that you don't feel the need for verbal confrontation speaks volumes about how grounded you are in your own truths and values. You don't need to win an argument. You don't need for someone to know that you're right. You simply choose to walk on in silence and let them think what they want.

Understanding that you don't have to verbally engage in a situation for your message to speak volumes is golden and one of the smartest tactics you'll ever use. A quick tip? If you are feeling unsure or confused about what to say in the moment, silence is a great way to give yourself some extra time to think it through before you say something you might regret. Just like picking your battles, as you become more assertive, it will be easier to determine which situations deserve your words or simply that sweet sound of silence.

Taking a Leadership Role

I never thought of myself as a leader while I was growing up, or even as an adult while I was in the work force. Leaders were people who had it all together and knew what they were doing. They could be called upon to take charge with any situation and under circumstances and were capable of heroic actions and results.

My belief system told me that leaders were born and not created because they wanted to be in charge and make the hard decisions that cross our paths regularly throughout our lives.

Then, I came online in 2006 as an entrepreneur and began to hear about people referred to as "thought leaders" and I began to think and take action differently.

A thought leader was simply sharing their experiences with others, and in a way that makes sense for those struggling with similar issues. It turns out that we all have much more in common than we could ever have imagined, and when I thought of it in this way my natural leadership abilities began to emerge and eventually to help me shine as I began this process of self-directing my life.

You may have seen either the original or the remake of a film called "True Grit", a western that starred John Wayne as U.S. Marshall Rooster Cogburn in the 1969 version and Jeff Bridges in the starring role in the 2010 remake. The plot involves a young girl wanting to hire Cogburn to find the man who killed her father. When asked why

Marshall Cogburn is the only person she wants for this job, she answers that she has heard that he has "true grit". I think of people who have the leadership traits of integrity and strong character as ones having true grit.

Being a gritty person means that you stick to your goals despite numerous issues, problems, setbacks and failures. The person has firmness of mind, determination, and unyielding courage. Are you a person of "true grit"? This continues to be a goal of mine and one that I focus on with every action that I take each day.

Being an entrepreneur requires a certain inner strength that I did not possess during the more than twenty years I worked as a real estate broker and appraiser and also as a classroom teacher.

Perhaps these traits and characteristics were always present inside of me, but seldom did I find the courage to bring them to the surface in any form. It was only when I came online in 2006 and discovered that it was entirely up to me to make things happen in my life and business that my character began to develop.

Think about the way you go about your daily life. You may think of yourself as being an honest person, but do you live in integrity? These are two separate things, I believe.

Living in integrity requires you to go above and beyond when it comes to dealing with and interacting with other people. It means that you go that extra mile to make sure the right thing is done. It also means that you seek out solutions to problems, both your own and those of people around you who can use your help and look for ways to not only solve problems but to enhance the situations you encounter so that true growth occurs. This is a tall order, but one that everyone can embrace.

These days I am someone others look to when they have questions, issues, and concerns around their everyday lives. Recently a friend's husband contacted me to ask my opinion on a job change he was considering. He told me that he and his wife had discussed it and that they had come to the conclusion that I was the person to discuss this situation with so they would have the best chance of success.

On that day, I realized that I had manifested the life I had wanted. My life's work is to assist others in their decisions, specifically around entrepreneurship and more generally with their lives. This type of leadership is possible when you focus on your goals and dreams each and every day.

Most recently, I felt like a leader within the group I am a part of with my intermittent fasting practice and longevity program. I led by example, so now it is more important than ever to show the others that even if we get off track for a period of time, it's possible to reinvent ourselves in a way that will make the journey an even more meaningful one.

Leaders Are Accountable... To Themselves, to Their Life's Work, and to Others

When things go awry — and they do — some people respond with lying, denying or minimizing their own responsibility.

Leaders know that to be respected or trusted they must be accountable. They must be willing to be responsible even before they know how things will turn out. I like the phrase,

If it is to be, it's up to me.

- ☀ Accountability starts with you. It means you are responsible. It's not so much a way of thinking as a way of being, and it starts from within.

- ☀ Accountability is about being reliable. Ask yourself, "Can people count on me to do what I say I'll do, and as I said I would do it?" You must always keep your word.

27

- Accountability is ownership. It's the willingness to hold yourself to account, it means taking total ownership no matter the mess up.

- Accountability is about creating clarity. When you are accountable you clear up the gaps and voids of expectations and what you are going to be doing.

- Accountability is about trustworthiness. When you are responsible and you make a commitment, you hold yourself to a high standard where others know and can trust in you.

- Accountability is a partnership. Partnerships are about support and mutual accountability; when you are held accountable by a partner, it's important to recognize and respect the power of their intention and respond with appreciation rather than anger.

Successful leaders front load accountability into their leadership development. Being accountable begins with accepting responsibility and leading from a place of action.

- Choices, paired with Behaviors and facilitated with Actions = Accountability
- I am accountable means you are able to count on me: if it is to be, it's up to me. Great leaders who are bound by their word are liberated by their accountability.
- Lead From Within: You are the leader of your life. Consider the importance of accountability and work to incorporate it in every area you influence.

Living in a self-directed way elevates your life experience in every moment. What areas do you need to work on and how will you take the next steps to live your best life and be a role model to others?

Chapter Three

A New Paradigm

"Until you make the unconscious conscious, it will direct your life and you will call it fate." ~ Carl Jung

To begin this journey of living a self-directed life, you must first do the work of shifting your mindset. This will lead you to a new paradigm and I encourage you to take the time to gift yourself a new way of thinking about your circumstances.

We all do an excellent job of telling ourselves stories, most of which are not true and simply based in fear, self-doubt, and indecisiveness. I realize while I am writing this that my words may seem harsh and judgmental.

But rest assured that everything I am sharing with you here is based in love and the belief that you can do anything you want to do in your life. You can also be and have anything you want, and practicing this belief system is the first step towards great joy and success in your life.

Mindset Shifts for the New Millennium

Let's begin with a discussion of what I mean by mindset shifts for the new millennium. Think about how the majority of younger people approach life. They are confident that they can do anything, and sometimes this level of confidence can lead to missteps. But for the most part, I love how positive people in their twenties are when it comes to feeling capable of achieving their goals and dreams.

I had this same type of confidence and belief in myself during my college years and the following years where I was just entering the work force.

But, along the way I began to lose my focus, and soon I found myself doubting and second guessing every move and decision I was about to make.

It may have been a new millennium, but I continued to be stuck in my old beliefs and feelings of inadequacy, fear, and poverty. I so wanted a new life, but at that time I had not a clue as to where I would even begin. I did what I always tended to do, which was to go to the library and search for answers in the books and other materials that were available.

The public library issued a "teacher" card to everyone who could show identification that proved you were an employee of the school district. That allowed me to take out books for the classroom, separately from ones for my personal use. On a balmy Saturday in November of 2004, I checked out more than a dozen books on a variety of topics, including ones from people who had changed their lives in various ways and had written a book to chronicle their experiences.

The one that made the difference for me was from Eckhart Tolle and titled *The Power of Now: A Guide to Spiritual Enlightenment*. I'm not exactly sure why I was drawn to this book, but perhaps it was what I read on the back cover of his book that resonated with me.

One night in 1977, at the age of 29, after having suffered from long periods of depression, Tolle said he experienced an "inner transformation". That night, he awakened from his sleep, suffering from feelings of depression that were "almost unbearable," but then experienced a life-changing epiphany. Recounting the experience, he said,

"I couldn't live with myself any longer. And in this a question arose without an answer: who is the 'I' that cannot live with the self? What is the self? I felt drawn into a void! I didn't know at the time that what really happened was the mind-made self, with its heaviness, its problems, that lives between the unsatisfying past and the fearful future, collapsed. It dissolved. The next morning, I woke up and everything was so peaceful. The peace was there because there was no self. Just a sense of presence or "beingness," just observing and watching."

Tolle recalled going out for a walk in London the next morning, and finding that "everything was miraculous, deeply peaceful. Even the traffic. The feeling continued, and he began to feel a strong underlying sense of peace in any situation.

I knew nothing of the spiritual concepts he was referring to, yet I knew that his book and teachings could open up my mind to new realities, beliefs, and experiences. I began reading and taking notes so that I could better understand what he was sharing.

I devoted an hour every weekday evening, and during the early morning hours on the weekends to reading, writing, studying, and internalizing Tolle's book. I renewed it twice at the library. By the spring of 2005 I was feeling more positive and uplifted in my daily life, but still had no answers as to what my next steps could be.

Then, on a Saturday morning in April, I awoke to a new day feeling as though something was different. It was as if the colors in my bedroom were brighter, the sounds coming from outside my window more clear and defined, and as I got up out of bed even the blanket and the skin on my arms felt different.

I wasn't afraid, but I knew something had shifted inside of me for me to feel this way. As I walked my dog down the street, every one of my senses was magnified amplified, and bigger than life. I was beginning my transformation, and with it my reinvention into the new life I so wanted to experience and live.

31

Reinvention in the Most Original Way

During the next few weeks, I found myself humming a familiar song and within the next day or two, that song would come on the radio in my car or be part of a television show or movie I was watching. Yes, this could have all been by coincidence, but it certainly didn't feel that way to me. This was magic of the best kind, for it was making me feel that anything was possible in my life. I hadn't felt that way in as long as I could remember and I was going along with it to see where it would take me.

I was most definitely ready to reinvent my life when I made the conscious decision to resign from my classroom teaching job I'd had for twenty years with the Los Angeles School District, as well as choosing to give away my longest and most reliable real estate clients. But the thing was… I had no idea what it even meant to reinvent my life.

Soon, I would learn all about reinvention, and how to do it in an original way that was custom-made just for me.

It was 2006, and the movie *The Secret* had just been released. I just happened to hear about it when I visited a Unitarian church in the new community of Santa Clarita, California I had recently moved to, as another part of my reinvention.

They invited me to see the movie at someone's home one evening and I was excited to be a part of something that was getting lots of buzz in the news.

During the film, I was introduced to Joe Vitale. He shared that we had the power within us to shift from a paradigm of scarcity in which you have "not enough" of the things you want and need to a paradigm of abundance in which you have more than enough of everything, all of the time. I was all in on this thinking and it was as if I could feel the earth moving beneath my feet as I walked to my car after the film ended.

Over the next several weeks, I began to question my own beliefs and values around health, wealth, and prosperity. I found it interesting that the people at the church were sinking further into despair after viewing the film, while I was feeling uplifted and inspired to learn more and to do the work in order to make some changes in my life.

I began to explore other ways to nourish my soul and found myself getting involved with service organizations and non-profits as a way to serve and to connect with more people in my new community, and this felt right for me.

Believing in the Possibilities

I'm going to share a story with you here, as I do regularly with all of the special people in my life…

Over a weekend decades ago I came to believe in magic. It happened when I fell in love with a book, and with reading and the experience would shape my thinking and turn me into the person I am today.

Every time I decide to gift a copy of this book to someone special in my life, I spend the weekend before rereading it from cover to cover. The title is Carbonel and it was written the year I was born by Barbara Sleigh.

She was a British author and when the children's librarian recommended it to me during one of my regular Saturday visits it did not seem to be something I would be interested in reading. But I trusted Mrs. Keene implicitly and checked out the book before I even opened it.

I will preface this story by saying that I was in the fourth grade at the time, and had just that week encountered my first bully at school. It was a girl in my class who had come to our school as a new student after the Christmas break. Sue was loud and rude and unlike anyone I had met up until that time. She would ultimately be asked to leave our school after cursing at one of the teachers, but that would be several months after she arrived.

Bullies rule by intimidation. They poke fun at others as a way to take the spotlight off their own shortcomings. Weaker personalities are drawn to these people because they believe they will be protected from the harshness of the world if they are loyal and support the bullies cause and agenda.

During the first encounter I had with Sue, she made a face at me on the yard during our physical education class. Then she stepped back, put her hands on her hips and said in a high- pitched voice that could be heard all over the playground, "What's your name, fatso?"

I turned and walked away, attempting to escape her cruel remark and any further wrath. But Sue followed after me. My face was red and my stomach began to ache. It felt like I was going to cry but I was trying with all of my might to keep that from happening. I silently prayed that no one else had heard what she had said.

A couple of the boys laughed and it was only because Mr. Carter, the P.E. Coach blew his whistle for us to stop playing and get in line that this episode was defused. And I didn't even think about until much later the fact that not one kid stood up to her for saying this for me. Perhaps that kid could have been me but her action took me by surprise and threw me off guard.

Looking back over my life, this was a turning point in how I perceived myself and in my level of confidence. I spent many decades blaming this girl, and everyone else who was present that day, until I finally realized it was me who was responsible for everything that occurred after those four words were spoken and sent out into the universe.

That evening at home, I had almost forgotten what happened until it was time to eat dinner. My mother served me a plate of food that included a ground beef patty, mashed potatoes, and peas. This was my favorite meal at that time, subject to change without notice.

And even though the ground meat came from a plastic tube, the potatoes were instant from a box of flakes, and the peas were the canned variety, I thoroughly enjoyed each bite. So much so, that after my plate was clean, I asked for more.

My mother motioned for me to help myself in the kitchen and the second plate had even more food on it than the first. This would mark the beginning of my overeating, stuffing my feelings down with food so that the pain would subside.

Before I went to bed, I stood in front of the full-length mirror on the door leading into our small bathroom. Yes, I was overweight. I heard her words again now, as clearly as when she had said them to my face. I felt sorry for myself but wasn't at all sure what I could have said back to her. I wasn't a mean girl and would never have said anything to hurt her feelings. What did the other kids do under these circumstances?

I wanted to tell on her to my mother. That wasn't going to happen because I had already begun protecting her from the world. Mom was a sensitive and creative person and she and I were pretty much alone in the world. There were a few elderly relatives back in her home state of Missouri, but I had only met two of them and didn't feel a connection with them on any level. So, I didn't say a word and went to sleep to dream of better times.

When we returned home from the library on that particular Saturday afternoon, I sat down on my bed to think. Then I picked up the book and thumbed through the pages. It was longer than I had thought while Mrs. Keene was telling me about the story. Over three hundred pages!

I had never heard of a chapter book this long. Even though I was in the "Red" reading group in my class (teachers always seem to think that kids can't figure out their secret codes) I thought this book might be too difficult for me. But I read a few pages and the next thing I knew it was time for dinner.

Quickly gobbling down my macaroni and cheese and salad, I escaped back to my reading corner. I was mesmerized by this book, not knowing quite why and found myself getting caught up in the characters, the setting, and the story that was unfolding.

The main character is a girl named Rosemary. She is about the age I was when I first read it. Rosemary lives in three rooms on the third floor of a house that has been broken up into several apartments with her mother, Mrs. Brown. This could have almost been my story in 1965. It was my mother and I living in one small apartment after another. Even though we lived in southern California, a 90-minute drive south to Disneyland and Rosemary lived with her mother in a section of London located about 5 kilometers north of London Bridge on the River Thames, our lives had many parallels.

Rosemary ends up with a black cat named Carbonel as her pet and confidant. I had a cat as well, a long-haired snow-white cat except for a splash of black at the tip of his tail and another spot on the tip of his nose. We called him Tippy and he was my best friend during my elementary school years because he listened to every word I said and consoled me when I was feeling down by snuggling up to me and purring loudly. Girls and their cats are capable of overcoming almost anything, it seems.

I won't share the adventures of Rosemary and Carbonel with you and spoil the story. But I will say that as I continued reading the book that weekend, at all hours and in an assortment of locations inside and out, something powerful shifted in my thinking and subconscious mind.

All of a sudden and out of the blue my world expanded around me and walls that had previously shut me out came tumbling down, exposing blue skies and sunshine.

Most important of all, I now believed in magic and knew deep in my core that everything I wanted in my life was possible. Believing in the possibilities of a world that had been so cruel to my mother and I was an awakening and revelation of great proportions.

Another item of interest I will share is that this was the longest chapter book I had ever seen, let alone read at that point in my life. Coming in at just over three hundred pages within twenty-five chapters it seemed overwhelming to me when Mrs. Keene had slipped it into my hands on that Saturday morning.

Even though I was an avid reader, I pretty much took the easy route by choosing to read books at or below my grade level, and many times ones I had read once or twice before. Perhaps it was a subconscious choice that kept me grounded in where I was rather than propelling myself further ahead. Staying in my comfort zone made my life simpler and easier to navigate. Leave it to Mrs. Keene, the librarian to gently persuade me to change, at least temporarily.

By Sunday evening I knew exactly what was going to happen in each chapter. Instead of losing interest I chose to read every detail as though I was reading through a transcript of a documentary that had transpired in front of my eyes at some point in the past. My favorite passage in the one in which Rosemary says the "summoning words" and Carbonel does not move a muscle. Then he steps down and comes toward her, purring loudly. She is overjoyed that he came to her when he didn't have to and Carbonel says,

> *"I came in gratitude. That will be a stronger bond than any spell."*

And so, it is, that we all find joy and fulfillment from doing what we are grateful for rather than that for which we feel obligated to do. Lead with your feelings of gratitude and happiness will be yours.

Please take my word for it when I tell you that you possess great power. You have it within yourself to do anything you want to do or be or have. If I could transform from being a shy, introverted child with little confidence and low self-esteem to someone who believes in myself and the magic of positive thinking then you can do this and more.

Choosing exactly what you want will become the only obstacle you will encounter. Belief in this power I think of as magic, and with believing in the possibilities comes great responsibility and dreams fulfilled.

I am a believer of magic and possibilities and everything positive life has to offer. Come along with me, if you will as I continue to share with you how a self-directed life could possibly change everything you ever thought was set in stone.

The truth is that navigating the world is a much more malleable process than any of us ever imagined it to be.

Schwartz Theory of Basic Values

This feels like the appropriate spot in this book to introduce you to Shalom H. Schwartz and his work around human values.

Schwartz is known among the circles he inhabits as a social psychologist, cross-cultural researcher, and creator of the *Theory of Basic Human Values*.

This theory he has developed and expanded upon over time recognizes universal values, which can be organized in four higher-order groups. Each of these universal values has a central goal that is the underlying motivator.

I am most interested in his work around self-direction, but I believe it is important to look at everything he is teaching, instead of simply extricating pieces of this theory as separate entities.

When we have autonomy, we are able to make our own decisions, control our own thoughts and bodies, go where we wish, and even be creative without fear of criticism or being prevented from doing so. It also implies we have the resources to do these things. In a democratic society this is a basic freedom, within the constraints of the law.

The first of the values is around openness to change, and includes self-direction as independent thought and action in choosing, creating, and exploring our human experience.

Schwartz's theory of basic human values identifies ten fundamental values that are shared across cultures and societies. Two of these values that relate to self-direction and universalism are:

Self-direction: This value refers to reliance upon one's own judgment and the pursuit of creative and independent thought and action. People who hold this value prioritize personal autonomy, innovation, and individuality over conformity and tradition. They tend to value freedom, curiosity, and self-expression and are often open to new experiences and ideas.

Universalism: This value reflects a concern for the welfare of all people and nature. People who prioritize universalism believe in equality, social justice, and protection of the environment. They are characterized by a willingness to transcend boundaries of ethnicity, race, religion, and nationality to promote the greater good.

Schwartz's theory suggests that these values are related to each other in a hierarchical way, with some values being more fundamental or basic than others. For example, self-direction is considered a more basic value than universalism, and individuals who prioritize self-direction may be more likely to also prioritize universalism.

Overall, the values of self-direction and universalism reflect a belief in personal autonomy and a comfort with diversity, both in terms of individuality and in terms of different cultures and perspectives. They are important values that help to shape how people see themselves and their place in the world, as well as their attitudes towards others and the environment.

Self-Direction... Defining goal: independent thought and action-choosing, creating, exploring. Self-direction derives from organismic needs for control and mastery.

He restricts the term "value" to broad motivational goals. Schwartz sees values as stable standards by which we evaluate everything else, including the appropriateness of any norms, attitudes, traits, or virtues that may be suggested to us.

Each basic value is described in terms of its motivational goal. A set of more specific values that express the basic value is given in parentheses after each description.

Benevolence: Preservation and enhancement of the people with whom one is in frequent personal contact: meaning especially family. Descriptors include helpful, honest, forgiving, responsible, true friendship, mature love.

Universalism: Understanding, appreciation, tolerance, and protection for the welfare of all people and for nature. Descriptors include broadminded, social justice, equality, world at peace, world of beauty, unity with nature, wisdom, protecting the environment.

Self-Direction: Independent thought and action… choosing, creating, exploring. Descriptors include creativity, freedom, choosing own goals, curious, independent.

In relation to self-direction, there is also Stimulation and Self-direction - intrinsic interest in novelty and mastery and Self-direction and Universalism - reliance upon one's own judgement and comfort with the diversity of existence.

Security: Safety, harmony, and stability of society, of relationships, and of self. Descriptors include social order, family security, national security, clean, reciprocation of favors, healthy, sense of belonging.

Conformity: Restraint of actions, inclinations, and impulses likely to upset or harm others and violate expectations or norms. Descriptors include obedient, self-discipline, politeness, honoring parents and elders.

Hedonism: Pleasure or sensuous gratification for oneself. Descriptors include pleasure, enjoying life, self-indulgent.

Achievement: Personal success through demonstrating competence according to social standards. Descriptors include ambitious, successful, capable, influential.

Tradition: Respect, commitment, and acceptance of the customs and ideas that one's culture or religion provides. Descriptors include respect for tradition, humble, devout, accepting my portion in life.

Stimulation: Excitement, novelty, and challenge in life. Descriptors include a varied life, an exciting life, daring.

Power: Social status and prestige, control or dominance over people and resources. Descriptors include authority, wealth, social power, social recognition, preserving my public image.

Happiness is not represented on Schwartz's list, either of basic or specific values, because Schwartz sees happiness as being the result of attaining one's values.

While I am still in the process of internalizing what Schwartz has created as his life's work, I thought it would be valuable to share what I've read and researched so far with you here. Perhaps your insight will make a difference, and the butterfly effect will be far reaching.

Section Two

Why You, Why Now?

"Belonging is best created when we join other people in producing something that makes a place better."

~ Peter Block

As I've already shared, my belief system kept me stuck in a reality that simply wasn't true for far too long. Other people lived the life they wanted, deserved the very best life has to offer, and achieved all of their goals and dream, effortlessly and with the most awesome outcomes.

Then one day, I decided that not only was I one of these "other people" but that everyone on planet Earth was endowed with these same gifts, talents, abilities, and characteristics.

As humans, we all have much more in common than anything that makes us different. We even have things in common with our animal friends!

So, why shouldn't you, right now go after the life you want? There is no reason why not, and so many reasons why this moment is yours. Demand the best, and be willing to step up to the plate and take a powerful and motivated swing. You, in this moment in time when you are reading this sentence, are ready for the greatness that lies within you.

As I've stated in the title of this book , when you learn about, embrace, and commit to living a self-directed life, all you need to do is to inspire, motivate, and empower yourself to this greatness that is already a part of who you are and have always been.

Let's move forward together, shall we? Your cape and chariot await, along with a bottle of spring water...

Chapter Four

Service Above Self

"A mind, once stretched by a new idea, never regains its original dimensions."

~ Oliver Wendell Holmes

Soon after coming online to start my new business, I became a Rotarian. I had never been a part of any group, and joining an international service organization was a big leap of faith for me.

I had so many questions, and the members not only had answers, but more questions for me. Rotary's motto is "Service Above Self" and as I embraced the deeper meaning of what this would mean in my life, I learned more about myself on a much deeper level than I had ever thought possible.

Who Are You, and What Do You Want?

Most people don't get what they want in their life for one simple reason: They don't know what they want! Looking back on my life over the years leading up to when I resigned from my classroom teaching job and gave away my best real estate clients in favor of coming online to start my business, I realized that I had no idea what lifestyle I wanted to create for myself.

The teachers played the lottery every week as a group, and there was no way I was going to let them win without me. Every Wednesday I put in my two dollars and for just a minute or two I dreamed of what it would be like to win. I would quit my job at the end of the school year, stop selling real estate and driving so many hours to do appraisals, and I would buy a new car. Oh yes, I'd take a vacation somewhere, but I wasn't sure where I'd go.

Looking back, my dream was lacking in so many ways, yet I could not possibly see past that thinking because of the way I was living at that time. It was more about surviving than thriving, and never about stretching outside of my comfort zone to play a bigger game. No, I was playing small out of necessity, and not even imagining anything more.

It turns out lottery winners have similar dreams of quitting their job, buying a new car, and taking a vacation. Yet, the overwhelming majority of them are right back where they started from after a few years, and their relationships with family members and friends are strained. It turns out a million dollars doesn't come close to buying the happiness and security we crave.

When I found out people just like me were starting businesses on the internet that could be run exclusively from a home computer, I wanted to know more. In April of 2005 I attended a real estate conference at the Los Angeles Convention Center, and stumbled into a breakout room where Raymond Aaron was speaking. A little more than an hour later, I was carrying a box of notebooks, cassette tapes, and other assorted items out to my car. I was ready to live what Raymond had described as "the mentored life" and nothing would ever be the same in my life experience.

Oliver Wendell Holmes told us that "A mind, once stretched by a new idea, never regains its original dimensions." That's what happened to me on that day, and it wasn't long before I knew more specifically what I wanted in my life, and I began connecting with the exact people and resources that would bring my dreams to life.

With Raymond's help, I began planning what I needed to do in order to resign from teaching at the end of June, 2006, just over a year away.

I asked people I knew to connect me with anyone they knew who had changed their life completely, such as leaving a job or a career and starting to do something entirely different in order to have a life that was more satisfying. Sure enough, two of my friends each knew people who had successfully changed their lives and we were introduced.

One couple invited me to go hiking with them on Sunday mornings. They took me to their house and showed me the inside of the pantry and the refrigerator. Their transformation was one that included a complete makeover with their eating as well.

Then they took me to the Agape church in Los Angeles, where we went to the bookstore after the service and they picked out several books for me to buy.

I didn't know it at the time, but within a few short months my life had been changed at the cellular level. I would never again feel like the life I wanted and deserved had passed me by. Instead, I realized that I could have and achieve anything I wanted.

On the first day of July, 2005, I began my new life as an online entrepreneur, and now I am dedicating my life to helping others to do the same or something similar.

What about you? What do you want? I mean *really want* your life to be, because your thoughts and actions do make a difference in every moment as to how your life is unfolding in front of your eyes.

I used to believe that part of the reason I was struggling in my life in many areas was because I didn't know the right people. It seemed to me as though others had inside information about everything because they knew the exact people who could help them.

Who do you know right now? Who would you like to know? I shared earlier that when I was ready to change my life and made the conscious decision to change careers and the city where I was living, I asked for help. This was a rare occurrence for me at that time; now I ask for and receive help every single day and it is empowering.

This is the six degrees of separation concept, made famous in the 1993 film. Six degrees of separation is the idea that all people are six or fewer social connections away from each other. As a result, a chain of "friend of a friend" statements can be made to connect any two people in a maximum of six steps.

All people are six or fewer social connections away from each other. Even if you and I are living on different continents, have nothing obvious in common, and are decades apart in age, we are still just six degrees away from one another.

On the social media and networking platform LinkedIn, I am in the top 3% of most connected people there. I often use the "six degrees" analogy to impress upon people why they must connect with me there. If they want or need to connect with someone on LinkedIn. More than likely I am a 1st or 2nd level connection to that exact person. This assumes all of us are on LinkedIn, while the concept of six degrees has no such requirement.

Reach out, connect, share, listen, and find the people whom you believe will be able to make a difference when it comes to getting what you want out of life. This works, and it's fun!

Showing Up... for Yourself and Others

I know a man, the son of a very close friend, who has not shown up for himself or for his children at any time during the almost twenty-five years I have been a part of his extended family.

His eldest daughter is from his first relationship and that girl's mother has always made it simple and easy for him to have a relationship with the child they brought into the world.

He remarried while this girl was still a toddler, and the new woman resented the fact that this child was a reminder that he had been previously married.

They have two daughters of their own. I am no longer able to visit them when I am in their city, as the stress and unhappiness is too much for me to bear.

So many situations have arisen over these years, and the last I heard, nothing has changed except that everyone involved is getting older. All three girls are now asking him to consider divorce, but perhaps even that will not be the answer.

I encourage you to make every effort to see your life as objectively as possible, and maintain some close friendships with people who will be honest with you.

Perhaps if I had done that, I would have been advised by others to leave my teaching job sooner. Instead, my perspective was limited at that time, and based in fear about how I would be able to replace that income.

These days, I show up for myself and others and know down deep in my soul that everything always works out with the best possible outcome and in a way that allows you to live well, and with grace and ease. My serving others, you are served as well.

What the World Needs Now

As I write this section, I'm thinking back to the spring of 1965, when I was in elementary school. The song that was popular at that time was "What the World Needs Now" and I had the 45. That's 45 rpm, or revolutions per minute if you remember back to those days.

Jackie DeShannon first sang this song, penned by Burt Bacharach and Hal David. It was actually about the controversy and disagreements among Americans about the Vietnam War.

But these days I relate it to more current events, like the eradication of Polio and bringing clean water to people in remote areas of the world. These are the two main projects that fuel the humanitarian efforts of Rotary International, a service organization I have been a member of since 2006. Clean water helps with eliminating polio in many areas, so these are definitely projects the world needs right now.

The pandemic reversed some of the work Rotarians had done over the years, so now we have doubled the efforts with additional financial resources and a partnership with the Bill and Melinda Gates Foundation, as well as a massive donation from Warren Buffett.

While this is great work that I am honored to play a small part in as an active member of Rotary and several other non-profits, there are many acts of kindness that are equally as important.

Each of us has within us the potential to help change and shape the world with our actions. Helping a child learn to read, assisting an elderly person at the grocery store, and listening to someone who is going through a painful time in their life are all opportunities for us to embrace the "Service Above Self" motto with rippling effects around our planet.

Chapter Five

Thinking Globally and Acting Locally

*"No matter who you are, how much privilege
you do or do not have, you can find a way to
give more to the world than you take."*

- Michael Bungay Stanier

The concept of thinking globally and acting locally is not a new one. It has been used in various contexts, including planning, environment, education, religion, mathematics, and business.

The "think global, act local" movement urges people to consider the health of the entire planet and to take action in their own communities and cities. Long before governments began enforcing environmental laws, individuals were coming together to protect habitats and the organisms that live within them.

This makes excellent sense, if you think about it. Growing up, I used to hear about people and situations in corners of the world far from where I was living, and wondered what good it would do for me to donate money or send food, clothing, or other items to them.

I didn't personally know anyone involved and lacked that feeling of connection that would have made it more likely for me to participate at any level.

But it did make sense for me to help with local causes because I could also see the progress and results with my own eyes.

Importance of Community

Until I resigned from my teaching position, gave away my longest and most reliable real estate clients, all while simultaneously building a new home and relocating to a community thirty miles north of where I'd lived for most of my life, I had never felt like I was a part of a community.

Sure, I had a post office and grocery store and bank and a neighborhood I was familiar with and people I knew by name, but to me it always felt like I was on my own.

When the Northridge earthquake struck on January 17th 1994, it was the middle of the night. I scooped up my dog Mickey, a tiny Yorkshire terrier who had been tossed halfway across the room, located my slippers, grabbed the flashlight I kept on the nightstand, and slowly made my way down the hallway and outside to my driveway.

The man from across the street called for me to help him, but I couldn't make out his words for the din of police cars, fire engines, and noises I couldn't make out.

I had grabbed my purse on my way out the door. I carefully placed Mickey inside and crossed the street.

Ron motioned me inside and once I crossed the threshold; I could see the mess. There was broken glass everywhere, their large dog was barking in the back yard, and their little girl, Sophia was crying in one of the bedrooms.

Without speaking, I followed him into the master bedroom and helped get his wife out of the hospital bed and into her wheelchair. Margie had been recently diagnosed with Lupus, an inflammatory disease caused when the immune system attacks its own tissues.

As he maneuvered the wheelchair out of the bedroom and down the hallway, I followed the sound of the crying and found three-year-old Sophia sitting up in her bed. I picked her up and met Ron in the hallway.

Placing Sophia in her mother's arms, I whispered "You're going to sit on mommy's lap."

We went to the driveway, and after locking down the wheelchair so it wouldn't move, Ron went to get their dog.

My little Mickey was beginning to struggle to get out of my purse, so as soon as he returned, I went back across the street to my house to get a collar and leash, as well as my list of names of people on our cul-de-sac and some flashlights and batteries.

I had lived here for less than a year, but I had become the Neighborhood Watch block captain right away. Someone had put up the sign on our street once I said I would do it, and I went door to door to introduce myself and exchange names and contact information.

At the time, it seemed to be the right thing to do, and I was also still working actively on a part-time basis with my real estate business.

Looking back, I know this was a pivotal moment where I stepped up to be a leader and to be involved locally with something that was an issue nationally in terms of safety and awareness as a way to deter crime.

On this day, I went to all fifteen of the houses to make sure everyone was alright. I gave out all of the flashlights I had, along with the extra batteries, and invited each person to find something to sit on so they could join us in the driveway.

It was four-thirty in the morning when the earthquake struck. As we watched the sun come up that morning, I was comforted by knowing that I was not alone.

What surprised me most was that almost all of my new neighbors had lived on the cul-de-sac for twenty years or more. Yet, few of them had spoken in many years, let alone spend time together to catch up with one another. The importance of community can never be over-stated, I believe.

Seeing It From the Local Perspective

What makes your neighborhood and community different from every other in the world? Well, for one thing... you live there!

Continuing with the earthquake as an example, I would say that our neighborhood was unique in that over ninety percent of the residents had lived in their homes since that tract was built in 1965. For the most part, their children had gone to school together from pre-school through high school.

At some point, they lost contact except for the occasional greeting when out for a run or to walk a dog, and also a wave when they drove into or out of the cul-de-sac.

Wouldn't it have been wonderful if some of them had deepened their relationships in some way? I'm imagining a vacation together, or starting a business or a non-profit organization, or perhaps volunteering for a cause they were mutually interested in.

I discovered over the next twelve years that none of these things had occurred, and no one could tell me why.

Being a Part of the Solution

When I first worked as a real estate appraiser, I was in an office run by a man named John. He had a paper sign affixed above his desk that said,

> *Don't be a part of the problem; be a part of the solution.*

When one of us would come to his office with a question that he knew we could solve on our own, he would simply point to the sign, and then go back to what he had been working on.

I quickly learned that solving my own problems and answering my own questions was a valuable skill, and this freed up space to save anything I wanted his help with more specifically for a special conversation later on in the day.

Your question at this point in my writing might be around self-direction, and how leading a self-directed life may be the result of the experiences we have had leading up to today.

Once I became focused on a self-directed path for myself, I looked for opportunities to connect with people of all ages, backgrounds, and walks of life. I am able to find inspiration and motivation in the words and actions of people around me. This becomes a smorgasbord that I may visit on demand, knowing that even if we are a continent or an ocean apart, we most likely have more in common that would bring us together than differences that would tear us apart.

And, I have learned that we do not need to agree on everything someone else has embraced with their thinking and actions. Having a set of core values to draw upon makes it even more likely that we will continue to find and use our voice to further the important conversations, projects, and goals that are meaningful to us.

Section Three

What Can You Expect If You Become Self-Directed?

"When you change the way you look at things, the things you look at change."

- Wayne Dyer

As you continue making your way through this book, you will want to stop and ask yourself regularly, "What's in it for me?" In the world of business, this is our WIIFM statement and makes all the difference.

Although I'm not attempting to sell you anything, and there is no pressing issue I am eagerly awaiting to recruit you for help with achieving, I do want you to begin seeing and hearing the world around you through a new and improved lens.

The Wayne Dyer quote, above, was my initiation into this new way of living. Yet, it would take me a few more decades to internalize what he was saying and self-direct myself to a lifestyle by design and clawing back my dreams for the future to the present day.

I have found this exercise to be helpful with the people around me:

I first ask them to think about something that happened in their life that made them stop and say "Hmm."

This exclamation is used to reflect hesitation or reflection and you may or may not say it out loud.

I like to think of these occurrences as a special kind of magic I can conjure up on a regular basis.

Perhaps it's finding a parking space right in front of the store, or hearing from someone just as you were thinking of them.

Or, it could be getting that raise or promotion, being accepted into a college, university, or program that you had already talked yourself out of because you were sure they would not select you as their top choice.

I'll address all of this and more in this section and encourage you to read, practice, and review your experiences as they unfold.

Chapter Six

Lifestyle by Design

"You are perfectly cast in your life. I can't imagine anyone but you in the role. Go play."

~ Lin-Manuel Miranda

Since 2006, I have lived what is referred to as a *lifestyle by design*. This means that I do not answer to a boss or a supervisor, there is no need to ask anyone's permission to take time away from my work, and I do not participate in recessions or downturns in the economy.

Though I'm not an island and wouldn't pretend to be, I do call the shots and make the decisions regarding how and where I live and lead my life.

You can do the same, but only after you have committed to doing whatever it takes to make your dreams come true, and seeking out the hard work that will set you apart from those searching for the easy button.

The Value in Change and Momentum

The only constant is change, as the saying goes, and once I learned how to welcome the life changes that would occur without my request, efforts, or permission my whole life changed.

I was the person who strived to micro-manage every situation so that I would always be prepared and never be surprised by what came my way.

Just using the words *always* and *never* set in place a culture of constraints around anything you wish to achieve.

The Theory of Constraints is actually a respected methodology for identifying the most important limiting factor that stands in the way of achieving a goal, and then systematically improving that constraint until it is no longer the limiting factor.

This theory was developed by Dr. Eliyahu Goldratt in the early 1980s. He shared it with the world and gained a massive following when he published his bestselling book on this topic, titled The Goal.

What constraints are you knowingly placing on yourself? Think about the momentum required to complete a task using physical labor. Over my lifetime I have mowed lawns, scraped barnacles off of wooden boats, cleaned houses to ready them for tenants, and assisted in the building of a children's sandbox, just to name a few. In each case, I initially placed constraints on myself that included negative affirmations around my physical strength, level of interest, and ability to be able to complete the task.

Your Ideal Day

Describing your ideal day before you're ready to live it can be an exercise in futility. Frustrating as this exercise may be, it is still one of the fastest and most reliable methods of discovering what you don't want in your life.

That's right; by figuring out what we do not want as a part of our daily routine, we can more quickly get to the best part – choosing what you do want to experience each day.

You see, the part of our mind that is allowing us to choose our own adventure – remember those books? – is more advanced and ready to cooperate with us when we are weeding through the possible outcomes.

For example, where and how will you live once you are able to do this from anywhere in the world?

Quite by accident, I discovered my favorite city in which to live in the United States in February of 1986. I have always been a cinephile, so when I read the article in the Los Angeles Times about a new film festival, I cut out the article and called the number they provided for those who wished to have more information.

This festival was to be held in downtown Santa Barbara, with the films to be shown at four local theatres and also at the Santa Barbara Art Museum.

I was a new teacher that year, so I called my favorite substitute and asked her to take my class for the two days I would be gone. My lesson plans were detailed and easy to read and understand. She was excited to have this assignment, so I met my friend and we headed north along the Ventura freeway to arrive the night before it was set to begin.

To this point in time, the only thing I could relate to Santa Barbara was the intersection with the traffic signal at the corner of State Street and Cabrillo Boulevard. The only times I had driven through this area were when I was driving up to San Francisco or some other part of the Bay area.

But on this particular evening, we made a right turn at the light and drove into the heart of Santa Barbara. It was dark and I wasn't impressed by anything we saw. The hotel was less than a mile past the stores, restaurants, and movie theatres, also on State Street. We would be able to walk to any of the venues and get a better feel for what this place was really like. It wasn't until the next morning that I fell in love with this sleepy little town.

We had booked three nights at the Orange Tree Inn. The man behind the desk told us to get a good night's sleep and then come back to the office in the morning for the free tour. Wesley would become a friend that weekend after making our stay so memorable.

It turned out the hotel was on the original site of Santa Barbara's historic movie industry, the Flying A Studios.

In 1912, Allan Dwan, a top director, moved his group of actors from San Diego to Santa Barbara. From 1912 to 1919, Flying A made more than 1,200 films. They were mostly cowboy movies filmed just outside of the city and included Lon Chaney Sr., and Victor Fleming.

I saw so many films that weekend that I couldn't remember them all. I had the program and other details from the Film Festival itself, as well as brochures from all kinds of places nearby.

We also spent time at two different beaches, drove up and down the streets to see the homes and the people who lived there, and wondered out loud why everyone wasn't either at the movies or the beach that weekend.

By the time we drove the two and a half hours back to the Los Angeles area, I had silently committed to spending more time in Santa Barbara, and to finally living in this magical city on a full-time basis.

Designing the Future

Do you now have at least more of an idea of what your ideal day looks like, or could look like? I encourage you to make notes, draw pictures, doodle, daydream, and cut photos out of magazines. What appeals to you? What repels you? What does your future look, sound, feel, smell, and taste like?

This is how you begin to design your future and create a lifestyle by design that will surpass all of your biggest goals and wildest dreams in record time.

I set about to create constraints around my goals and dreams almost immediately. I told myself that I would not be able to get a teaching job in Santa Barbara because that district preferred teachers who were younger, more experienced, completely bilingual, and active in the community. That let off the hook because I was the opposite of most of those qualities. And who could blame me for not wanting to leave a sure thing and run after a pipedream.

It would be almost five years before I would return to Santa Barbara. When I did, it was for my work as a residential property appraiser.

The first home I appraised was a gated estate on three acres in the Montecito area, just south of Santa Barbara. I was stopped cold in my tracks as I exited my car and walked around to find someone to speak with and ended up face to face with a creek.

The babbling brook looked as though it was straight out of a fairy tale and I stepped away for a moment to catch my breath. Once I did, I moved closer and saw some small fish swimming by without a care in the world. Evidently, there were no fisherman nearby.

This had to be the most beautiful and serene setting I had ever experienced. I made myself snap out of my trance so I could get back to the work I was assigned to do on that day.

I finally heard some voices. Walking carefully back up the pathway, I followed the sounds to a guest cottage. As I lifted my hand to knock, the door opened and a woman smiled at me.

"Hello, you must be the appraiser. Did you have any trouble finding it? Where are my manners? What's your name? Would you like something to drink? I'm Diane."

She was tall and wearing mostly black clothing, with gold bracelets and earrings and necklaces to finish the look.

I smiled back.

"Yes, I mean no, it was pretty easy to find. I'm Connie Green. I stopped back in Summerland at the park and had my lunch. I was early because I didn't know how long it would take me from the Valley."

"The valley?" She looked puzzled and cocked her head to one side.

"The San Fernando Valley. I'm in Chatsworth."

"I'm sorry, I don't know it.

As we walked down the steps and onto the stone path our conversation moved to things not so related to real estate. I asked her what she did, and when she told me she was an interior designer she could tell that my mood had shifted.

She asked me if everything was alright and I opened up to her about my dream of moving to Santa Barbara someday.

She listened as I talked about my life as a full-time classroom teacher and also working in real estate on a part-time basis. I told her that anytime I met someone with any connection to Santa Barbara, they always seemed to be in the creative field. I had met writers of all kinds, from poets to screenwriters; fine artists; producers and directors; and now, an interior designer. I told her I wasn't creative at all, and that I had wanted to be a writer but didn't write very often.

She stopped, and for a minute we listened to the creek flowing, different types of birds singing, and a vehicle passing by on the road behind the property.

"What do you hear, and see, and feel? She asked me.

It was a trick question. "I don't know. The water moving downstream, and some birds, and a car." I motioned around me as I spoke.

"What do you *feel?*"

I thought for a moment. "I feel bad that I don't know what to do to have a different life. And I feel bad that I feel bad."

With that, we both laughed. Simultaneously, the sun shone brightly through the tall trees and there was a gentle breeze that made the branches and leaves sway gently.

"When you feel what you want to experience, it will move closer. It's not about being creative, which of course you are because everyone creates. It's not about money, or education, or knowing certain people. It's more about getting out of your head and allowing it all to happen. Once you can feel what you want your life to be like, those feelings will manifest into your reality."

I nodded, and soft tears welled up in my eyes. In that moment, I felt that Diane had imparted some wisdom to me I was not quite ready to understand and act upon. I felt happy, or at least joyous for this experience. And I felt like something more was possible for me.

Her words had landed on me in way that would forever change me, as all interactions and experiences do, when we allow them in fully.

I will never forget that day, and I know that even though it took years for me to take the next steps forward, everything unfolded in the perfect time and space for me. And I did make it to Santa Barbara as a resident, without giving up my life and home in Santa Clarita, and it is a wonderful and joyous experience.

Chapter Seven

Self-Direction in Real Time

"Joy does not simply happen to us. We have to choose joy and keep choosing it every day."

~ Henri Nouwen

There is always a place for theory, but not with what I'm choosing to share with you here. Instead, I'm going to tell you about simple life hacks that will allow you to shift your mindset and your focus in ways that will allow you to experience self-direction in real time.

Moment by moment, your awareness will grow and you'll become more confident with your life as it is right now, the changes you feel compelled to make, and the bigger picture of what you would like your life to look like.

Morning and Evening Routines

Your morning sets the tone for your day. You may already agree with this idea, but are you aware that your morning actually gets its start the evening before?

While creating and putting in place a morning routine will significantly improve your life, it's more effective if you front-load your morning about twelve hours earlier.

If you would have asked me years ago if I had a morning routine, I would have answered in the affirmative. During the more than twenty years I spent in the work force, before coming online as an entrepreneur, writer, and marketer in 2006, I did the same thing day after day. My mornings looked something like this:

- ☀ Jump out of bed when the alarm goes off at 4:30am
- ☀ Walk my dog
- ☀ Quickly shower and dress for the day
- ☀ Gulp down cereal, juice, and a banana
- ☀ Make my lunch
- ☀ Dash out the door by 5:45am
- ☀ Rush through my day, only to do it all over again the following morning

This was not an optimal or healthy morning routine on any level. It was simply the way I had structured my life up until that point, and it was not serving me. Now my life is very different and everything, I mean every. little. thing. about my life has changed, and it's entirely based on what I'm sharing here with you.

A morning routine puts intentionality into your day. It gives your morning form, design, and function. Imagine yourself traveling through each step, calm, cool, and collected. You know exactly what's needed of you and when. There are no surprises to leave you scrambling. Nor are you likely to forget what's important. Your morning routine will strengthen your most important relationship – the one you have with yourself.

If it seems intimidating to form a routine to do all these things, take heart. Really, there are only a few steps you need to worry about to make your day come off without a hitch.

Understand What It's All About

Embarking on a new routine is hard work, especially as you work to build this routine into something which will be habitual. It's easy to go back to the old ways you've always done things, especially if you feel tired or discouraged.

This is why your first step involves understanding your purpose. Know why you're striving to have a better morning, and speak these words out loud every morning when you first get up to remind yourself of them. Are you looking for greater productivity? A calmer day? More confidence? You'll need to figure it out if you don't know before beginning.

Implement Your Routine in Baby Steps

You can't change around your entire sleep schedule or make profound changes about your mornings all at once without burning out quickly. This is why it's important to work out a plan in advance where you know what changes you are making and when.

For example, if you normally get up at 9:00am but would prefer to get up at 7:00, you'll want to make some small changes that work toward your goal. So, for the first week, you might get up at 8:45 and the week after 8:30, etc...

Commit to Consistency

You're not going to succeed in building new habits if you don't do the same thing repeatedly. Realize you can't do this in half measures. Commit to doing this routine every single day.

Work Out an Evening Routine

Your morning will go better if you use it with an evening routine that sets up a regular bedtime. You can also use evenings to do prep work for the next day, such as laying out your clothes and planning what you will take from your to-do list and move to your schedule for that following day.

Create Your Routine

The key to making your routine is to address all of your needs. Some things you might do for physical health (exercise, eat right) while others benefit you spiritually (meditate, pray), mentally (learn, self-talk), or emotionally (journal, affirmations). The goal is to bring yourself into harmonious balance every day.

Together these five steps will help you create the perfect morning routine. But what about meditation, visualization, and daydreaming as a part of your morning routine?

Using Visualization to Get What You Want in Life

What do you want out of life? More importantly, how do you intend to go about getting it?

We all have so many wants. Some are very simple, such as wanting to lose five pounds in time for swimsuit season. While others, such as changing to a new career, are more complex. What's interesting is that you can use the very same technique to get precisely what you want, whether your goal is big or small.

Visualization is the technique of picturing a goal in your mind in detail so that you can manifest this change in your life. Sound hard? Really, it's not. By following these five simple steps, you'll get exactly what you want in almost no time at all.

Engage Fully in the Vision

You absolutely must put yourself into the visualization as fully as you possibly can. Use all your senses and emotions to experience this vision in a way that is real to you. There can be no holding back here.

Experience Different Viewpoints

What does this visualization feel like to you? Experience it first as yourself so that you can connect emotions to actions. You want to feel every part of it. Now, step back and experience it again as if you're watching yourself succeed from outside of yourself, like watching a movie. Why? This helps you to see details you might miss otherwise.

Live the Success

When you're done with the visualization, it's time to live the part. Become the person you saw at the end of the vision. How does that person move? Think? Act?

Reinforce the Message

Visualization needs need back-up to be successful. The world is full of negative influences, some of them finding root in your own mind. Keep your self-talk positive, use affirmations, and look for ways to constantly reinforce the vision in your mind without tearing it down.

Make the Vision Tangible in a Way You can See it

Creating a dream board or collage will set out your visualization in a place where you are constantly reminded of the experience. Seeing it over and over will also reinforce your goals and strengthen your resolve.

By following these steps, you'll find you will find your dream becoming more and more solid. Of course, you're going to have to put in the work to achieve what you want. However, by using visualization, you get clear where you're going and how to get there.

Making Each Moment Count

In a busy world, we tend to rush from event to appointment to activity and back again, without taking the time to stop and smell the proverbial roses.

We've all been there, as the real world is typically not set up to make living a self-directed life a priority for anyone.

Instead, we go to school, take a job, perhaps move on to a career, have a family, relocate to a new city, get involved with activities around the people in our families and communities, and wake up one morning wondering what it's all about and why we feel like we have missed something.

I purposely structured the previous paragraph to make you feel like you needed to catch your breath, because that is exactly how it feels for almost everyone who insists on living in that manner. And yes, it *is* your choice.

The self-directed life gives you that room to breathe. Everything you do is thought about and planned, at least to some extent, in advance. You let go of being reactive to everything that comes your way, as though you're always in the middle of a video game and attempting to rack up more points than those you are playing against, or even along with.

Can you imagine the difference, just by what I've been sharing so far? I sincerely hope so.

My life was a roller coaster in that there was always more to do than time in which to do it. My routines and productivity were based on being able to accomplish the most tasks and activities in the least amount of time.

Taking a shower or walking the dog gave me a brief respite from the chaos, but only briefly. I was only able to take a one-week or 10-day vacation every other year because of time and money constraints, and that time flew by so quickly I sometimes had to look back at the photos to remember what I had experienced.

The self-directed life is one in which you do not need or even want a vacation from, because every day becomes one in which you are awash in satisfying experiences and with people who energize you, rather than the other way around.

Here's an experiment for you to try: Spend one full hour tracking what you are thinking and how you feel. Do this at a time when you are among people and free to move about and interact with others, the environment and nature, and at a time when you are feeling like you are ready to make a change in your life.

What do you notice? Perhaps you would prefer to be alone, or to only be with a specific person. Maybe something or someone is annoying you, or making you smile. Think about the location you are in very specifically, knowing that in each moment you always have the choice to make it more enjoyable for you, if only you believe this to be true.

This exercise is one I continue to do. We are all in a constant state of change and must listen to our mind and body as often and as carefully as possible.

Being Open and Willing to Change

Heraclitus told us the "the only constant is change and that everything changes and nothing remains still; and you cannot step twice into the same stream."

I shared earlier that I had fought successfully for my limitation of being resistant to change for decades, only to discover that change is not only to be revered, but also something to look forward to in our lives.

We only get out of something what we are willing to put into it. This goes for everything you can think of and imagine.

If you put in the time to practice a musical instrument or a sport, you'll improve.

I most recently in my life discovered it to be true with my writing, even though I had been told this by other writers and in many different ways for years. A professional television and screenwriter challenged me to write a new short story every day for ten days, saying that there would be very little chance the ninth and tenth stories wouldn't be noticeable better than the first couple of stories. Of course, he was correct.

Section Four

How Do You Become Self-Directed?

"Patience only works if you do. Doing the work + patience = results. Planning to work + patience = you're just waiting. Do the work."

- James Clear

Choosing to *self-direct* your life is much like creating a feature film. The subject of the film is you, first as a much younger person and then, over the course of the movie you become the person you are today.

We are all works in progress, and learning to self-direct will help you to jump start your progress significantly.

In my thinking and experience, much of what I'm sharing with you here is based on your mindset, and dependent upon whether you're living with a scarcity or an abundance mindset.

A Scarcity Mindset Can Hold You Back

A scarcity mindset will have you believing in limits. Time is limited. Money is limited. Even you are limited at what you can accomplish. It's like putting blinders on to everything good in the world and focusing only on the lack thereof. However, if you've never been conditioned to think any other way, it can be tricky to break the chains of a scarcity mindset.

For many people, life is just unfair. They don't see mindset as the cause of their problems and tend to blame forces outside their control. For this reason, having a scarcity mindset can hold you back long before you even realize what is happening.

Here are the five main areas where a scarcity mindset may be holding you back.

Confidence

A scarcity mindset will have you believing that you're never enough. You're not thin enough to wear a bikini. You're not smart enough to go for that new job. You avoid putting yourself out there or taking risks because you're too scared of what people will say. What if you look stupid? What if you fail?

Growth and change are impossible with this mentality because you won't allow yourself to move past your fears in order to realize your full potential.

Career/Money

Scarcity has you seeing obstacles, not opportunities, when it comes to career and money. You believe you have to scratch and claw and hustle your way to the top just so you can "get yours." You place a ceiling on how much money can come into your life because you think there's only so much to go around.

You think making any decent amount of money has to be difficult. This mindset will have you believing that everyone else is smarter or better or more qualified than you. It's hard for anyone living in scarcity to embrace change, take risks or step very far outside their comfort zone to experience anything new.

Relationships

When you live in scarcity, you are rooted in the fear that your choices are limited and there is not enough love to go around. You settle. You obsess. You stay stuck in unhealthy, toxic relationships for way too long or have an obsessively tight hold on someone which, in turn, causes them to leave.

You tend to place blame on others and find it hard to compromise, an important component of a successful relationship. Professional relationships can also be strained because of your overly competitive nature and inability to share credit or recognition.

Health/Wellness

When a scarcity mindset is in control, it has a big impact on your physical and emotional wellbeing. Not only are stress and anxiety a part of your daily life, you make excuse after excuse as to why you can't lose weight, exercise more, or maintain a healthy eating plan.

Because you see it as a limited resource, you may have a tendency for overindulgence when it comes to food. You remind yourself of everything you will have to give up, rather than what you will be gaining by adopting a healthier lifestyle.

Productivity

Goal setting plays a big part in how productive you are, simply because you know what you are working towards. The problem is, when you live with a scarcity mindset, you lack the ability to set clear goals. Your future outlook is bleak, and you don't really feel like you are working for much more than a paycheck and the occasional raise.

Excuses are your friend. If you just had more time, more energy, more money THEN you could finally accomplish something. Rather than seeing it as a mindset issue, you blame others and your circumstances for your inability to get things done.

Living with a scarcity mindset can wreak havoc on your life without you even realizing what the true problem is. Becoming aware that you need to break free of these limitations is so important to your current and future success.

Do you ever look around and wonder how other people succeed in life and you just feel like a failure? You don't understand why you can't get a better job, make more money, be happier, more confident and have better relationships. You tend to blame everything from your childhood to your circumstances, but it doesn't change the fact that you are stuck in a big rut.

So many people waste their lives blaming a crappy lot in life and never spend time looking inward to the source of the problem which is their mindset.

Our mindset is the sum of every thought, belief and opinion that has been passed down to us or learned through our own experience. It's the driving force behind our action or inaction and the one that we choose to adopt determines the path we take in life.

One path will have you Living in abundance and the other struggling in scarcity. The important thing is that YOU get to decide which path you choose. Which one will you place in the driver's seat?

Let's dig into the key differences between abundance and scarcity and see how they both impact your success…

Abundance Mindset

Here are a few ways that developing an abundance mindset will allow you to live a more fulfilled, exciting and successful life…

You Have More Than Enough

An abundance mindset revolves around the idea that there is plenty for everyone. Money, Time, Resources, Love, Opportunity, Success – it's all out there, ready and waiting for you (and everyone else) to take a piece of the pie.

Change is welcome

You understand that change is necessary for growth and will actively seek out opportunities to step outside your comfort zone and embrace new ventures in life and business. You look at failure as an opportunity to learn instead of giving up as soon as you hit the first obstacle.

You are Happy for Others

Rather than being threatened by another's good fortune, you are genuinely happy and supportive of someone else's success. You enjoy seeing others receive abundance in their life because you know there is more than enough to go around.

Optimistic Attitude

An optimistic, positive attitude is another attribute of someone who adopts this mentality. You see limitless possibilities in front of you and choose to have a positive outlook no matter what happens in life. You are able to move forward despite your circumstances and focus more on what is working and going well in life rather than what is not.

Practicing Gratitude

A huge part of an abundance mindset is the ability to practice gratitude on a daily basis. When you have a grateful heart it's easier to notice even the smallest blessings. You will tend to focus more on what you have then what you lack and always find something to be thankful for.

Scarcity Mindset

These are just a few ways that a scarcity mindset will hold you back and keep you from realizing your true potential.

Fear

A scarcity mindset keeps a person rooted in fear - fear of the unknown, fear of change, fear of the future. You may avoid taking risks and rarely leave your comfort zone because the possibility of failure is too strong. This can greatly impact your career choice as well as how much money you make.

Comparison Trap

You constantly feel the need to compare yourself to others when living with a scarcity mindset. You tend to base your self-worth entirely upon how well you measure up to everyone else. This is a lose-lose situation and a vicious cycle that will keep you from experiencing true connection with others.

Living in Lack

Scarcity will have you believing that there is a limit to everything – time, money, resources, opportunity, love and success. There is always a fear that there won't be enough and can lead to over-indulgence and competitiveness. Someone with this mindset will find it hard to share and give to others which can have a negative impact on relationships.

Jealousy/Envious of Others

You'll find it hard to be happy for others when you are living with a scarcity mindset. You feel threatened by other's success and celebrate when they fail only because you lack confidence in your own life and feel like success is never within your reach.

Pessimistic Attitude

With a scarcity mindset, you focus entirely on what wrong with your life and are stuck in a continuous pity party. Your outlook on the future is mediocre at best and you tend to be a "worst case scenario" type person. You see your current situation as permanent which impacts your ability to see any other opportunities.

Both abundance and scarcity have a huge impact on your life – It's easy to see which one is preferable between the two, however, it all depends on you. The first step is becoming aware of your thoughts and deciding which life you want to live.

Maintaining an Abundance Mindset

When you want to adopt a healthier lifestyle, it's normal for a person to develop an exercise regimen or meal plan so they can maintain their results. The same goes for a healthy mindset. Now that you've made the shift from scarcity to abundance, you want to maintain all the work you've done.

Find Your Tribe

Anytime you're attempting to make a life change, it's important to recognize who is in your corner. You want to surround yourself with abundance minded people who will support you in this journey to better your life. Make an effort to hang out with them on a regular basis. Fill your social media feed with people that you aspire to be, not the judgmental mom from down the street or the guy from high school who still lives in his parent's basement. Be intentional about who you spend time with and make sure they are filling a positive space in your circle of friends.

Give More

Get into the habit of giving something of yourself on a daily basis. It can be as simple as a kind word or a smile. Go through your house and donate things you don't want to someone in need.

Pay for someone's meal in the drive-through. Volunteer at a soup kitchen or the animal shelter. A random act of kindness may change someone's whole outlook and it will strengthen your hold on the abundance mindset you've worked so hard for. That's a win-win in my book.

Organize Your Life

When you feel like your life is in order, everything else tends to fall into place. If you're always running out of time, make a point to keep track of your day. See where your hours are being spent and then decide if you need to re-work some things in your schedule. Money issues?

Create a budget and outline everything you have coming in and everything you have going out. Declutter – your office, your social media accounts, your phone. Make space for the things that are really important.

Feed Your Mind

On any given day we are bombarded with negativity through news reports, social media, etc. Because of this, it's so important feed your mind positive, uplifting material every day in order to maintain a healthy mindset.

Reading books, listening to podcasts or Ted Talks, taking a class, learning a new skill – these are all great ways to keep your mind out of the scarcity gutter and focused more on abundance.

Self-Care

It may seem odd, but self-care and abundance go hand in hand. Life gets so hectic sometimes that we don't realize we are hanging by a thread until it gets ready to snap. It's important to recognize those needs and block out some time just for us.

Indulging in self-care doesn't always mean a pampering massage or getting a facial. I engage in a variety of activities, both by myself and with others to practice self-care every single day. This is a far cry from the way I lived my life before starting my online business and working from home in 2006.

It can be something as simple as going offline for a weekend or taking a warm bath. Make yourself a healthy meal or learn to say no more often when something doesn't serve you. A big part of abundance is self-love – what better way to strengthen your mind and take care of yourself in the process.

Create a routine that works with your schedule and do what feels right. As with anything, maintaining a healthy, abundance mindset takes work, but you'll love the end result.

When you've been locked into a scarcity mindset for so long, it may be intimidating to think about a mindset shift. However, moving from scarcity to abundance doesn't have to be difficult and it will end up being one of the most life-changing things you'll ever do.

You'll discover that as you move closer to creating and living a self-directed life, you begin to begin to realize that you've become your own self-help guru. I'll share more about that in this next chapter...

Chapter Eight

Becoming Your Own Self-Help Guru

"The only journey is the one within."

- Rainer Marie Rilke

My own journey of personal development and growth began deliberately in 2005. I had been teaching for almost twenty years, and working part-time in real estate for even longer. I so needed a change from what I was living each day and had no idea where to turn.

I just knew that I was exhausted, broke, and lonely much of the time. As my 50th birthday approached, I longed for answers to the questions I was pondering. I was also seeking out new questions to ask and people to discuss all of this with who had been where I was at that point in my life.

Decades earlier, my mother and others had attempted to introduce me to ideas and teachings that could have accelerated my progress, but I was not yet open to the concept and belief that my life could be changed from the inside out.

My mother had joined a group called the Rosicrucians while I was still in elementary school. Rosicrucians describe themselves as a community of philosophers who study what they consider to be Natural Laws in order to live in harmony with them. Their mission is to provide seekers with the spiritual wisdom necessary to experience their connectedness with the miraculous world around us and to develop Mastery of Life.

She studied their materials, signed up for lessons, and dragged me to any evening or weekend event where children were welcome to attend. My stubbornness with being open to their gentle and relevant wisdom finally won out, and by the time I was in junior high school my mother no longer discussed it with me.

So, I passed on this valuable upgrade and instead, I chose to learn my life lessons the old-fashioned way: I earned them by allowing just about everything to be onerous, burdensome, arduous, and just plain complicated.

It's interesting that as my mother was living the final two years of her life, I was just beginning to understand the value of self-improvement in my life. During her final days, we had conversations about life and death and everything in between that were deep and satisfying to us both. I am grateful to have had this time and those conversations with her before she passed.

Motivating Yourself Towards Greatness

Are you motivating yourself each day to achieve and accomplish the goals you've set for yourself? The answer to this question will guide your life's journey and change your life in untold ways.

I work with newer authors, marketers, and entrepreneurs and have discovered over almost two decades of mentoring that motivation must come from within.

While others can encourage, support, inspire, teach by example, and lead you in your quest for achieving goals and dreams, only you can push yourself over the top of any mountain by motivating yourself to greatness.

The questions you must ask yourself as you walk the path of the entrepreneur's journey also include... "What is my motivation for wanting to build and grow an online business?"

When I began mentoring people who were seeking out a life and business around online entrepreneurship, authorship, and marketing and teaching them my proven strategies based on my experiences, I mistakenly assumed that they were motivated in the same way I was at the time: to earn enough income online to be able to replace what I had been making as a classroom teacher and working part-time in real estate during the previous twenty years. Not so, with many people who were coming to me for mentoring telling me that it was different for them.

Instead, I soon learned that people's motivation for coming online included wanting to share a specific message with the world; having the desire to be a part of a community that was mostly online so they could step away from interacting in the physical world; and wanting to write a book to leave a legacy for their family and friends. This motivation is more intrinsic.

Intrinsic motivation is defined as the doing of an activity for its inherent satisfaction rather than for some separable consequence. When intrinsically motivated, a person is moved to act for the fun or challenge entailed rather than because of external products, pressures, or rewards.

Why am I sharing all of this with you today? Because I work best with people who are motivated to become authors, marketers, and online entrepreneurs in order to create multiple streams of income, with many of these being passive income streams.

Motivating Yourself is the First Step to Setting and Achieving Your Goals

Goal setting and achieving strategies were relatively new to me when I first began my online business in 2006. I had heard that writing down your goals, reviewing them regularly, and then "course correcting" as you got closer to implementing them would make a difference. But it would take the help of two mentors for me to actually internalize and then implement the power of these concepts.

Motivating yourself may seem like an insurmountable goal at first, but upon closer inspection you'll find that it can be satisfying to know that you alone are capable of motivating yourself to greatness. Here's a strategy I've used that may be helpful to you...

The Warren Buffet Strategy

This strategy has three steps:

Step 1: Write down your top twenty-five goals. This could be career goals, personal goals, weekly goals, annual goals, etc.)

Step 2: Go over your list and circle your top 5 goals. Make sure take some time with this part; don't rush it!

STOP – Do NOT proceed to Step 3 until you have done the two steps above first.

Step 3: Now you essentially have two lists: the circled items are List A, and the remaining items are List B. So logically the next thing to do is start on your most important tasks.

Well, not exactly. Here's the catch – Buffet says this, "Everything you didn't circle just became your Avoid-At-All-Costs list. No matter what, these things get no attention from you until you've succeeded with your *Top 5*."

For Step 3, you only want to focus on working on the items on List A.

Why this strategy works: Eliminating things you care about is the most difficult part of this productivity method.

Those twenty items on List B are things you care about, just like the items on List A. They are tasks that important to you for one reason or another. It's super easy to tell yourself that you're being productive while spending time on those twenty tasks. But when you hold them up to your top five goals, those other tasks are simply distractions from your biggest goals.

Spending your limited time on secondary priorities may just be the reason you still have twenty half-completed projects instead of five finished ones.

Motivating Yourself to Unlimited Income

Did you know that income is not all created equal? Like many people, I started with "earned" income when I was very young. This required me to work for an hour in exchange for being paid for that hour of my time. As a classroom teacher, I was salaried, meaning that I was paid a set amount every four weeks, no matter how many hours it took me to complete the work that needed to be done. The majority of people in the world are on the earned income model.

In real estate, I was on commission and paid when a transaction was completed. That was when I first learned about "portfolio" income, where you could invest in properties or stocks and bonds or something similar and then be paid on an ongoing basis without having to do any more work. The "catch" was that you had to come up with money to invest in order to get these streams of income in place and flowing.

When I came online in 2006, I quickly learned about "passive" and "residual" income, where you create something once and then get paid over and over again. This can be from information products, online courses, books, membership sites, and more. My goal is to help you to create something of value to others so you'll have income coming in 24/7/365. Affiliate marketing is a big part of this income strategy. This is what we refer to as the internet marketing lifestyle and it's easier than you may have imagined to set up.

Motivating yourself is a skill I encourage you to develop and practice. Think about your goals and the ways you would like to spend your time throughout each day. Perhaps you want to do more writing, or to travel, or to volunteer in your community. Whatever your dreams and goals may be, know that you can and will achieve them by maintaining focus and consistency in your daily life.

Walking a New Path

Walking a new path can be exciting, at least until you realize how much you do not know. Perhaps it's like a Kindergartner on the first day of school. They've anticipated this moment for so long, preparing in various ways, and finally arriving at the door of the classroom, only to realize they weren't prepared at all.

We are always surrounded by teachers. Only some of them are found at schools, as everyone is capable of teaching someone else what they know, and in a way that is perhaps more interesting and enticing to the learner.

I was not familiar with the concept of mentors in my life. It wasn't until I met Raymond Aaron the year before I came online that I understood what was meant by "living a mentored life." I've since written a book on this topic specifically, and once you have people to take you by the hand and guide you to the life you want and deserve, you will live this way forever. I encourage you to be open and excited about what I'm sharing with you here.

I consider this next section to be one of great importance to your life. All of us can relate to the concept of being more present and aware as we become more proficient in any given area, and this way of thinking will empower you to move to the next level more rapidly and with greater confidence.

Let's get started…

The Five Levels of Consciousness and Four Stages of Competence

"Consciousness is defined as everything of which we are aware at any given time - our thoughts, feelings, sensations, and perceptions of the external environment.

Physiological researchers have committed to a study of consciousness, in examining physiological rhythms, sleep, and altered states of consciousness.

There are five levels of consciousness:

- ☀ Conscious - sensing, perceiving, and choosing
- ☀ Preconscious - memories that we can access
- ☀ Unconscious - memories that we cannot access
- ☀ Non-conscious - bodily functions without sensation
- ☀ Subconscious - "inner child," self-image formed in early childhood

The 4 Stages of Competence

The 4 stages of competence, also known as the "conscious competence" learning model, were first introduced by Martin M. Broadwell in the 1960s. The model describes the process of acquiring new skills or knowledge and how individuals move from being unaware of their incompetence to becoming proficient.

I was greatly impacted by learning about this model. In my own journey, I was able to progress relatively quickly because I was open to understanding why I was at each level at the time, and patient with myself as I continued to progress, backslid once or twice, and then moved forward once again.

The four stages are as follows:

- 🔆 Unconscious incompetence: At this stage, individuals are not aware of their lack of knowledge or skills in a particular area. They may be ignorant or indifferent to the subject and may not see the need to learn more.
- 🔆 Conscious incompetence: At this stage, individuals become aware of their lack of knowledge or skills in a particular area. They may realize that they need to learn more and may seek out resources to help them improve.
- 🔆 Conscious competence: At this stage, individuals have acquired the knowledge or skills necessary to perform a task, but they must consciously focus and make an effort to apply them. The individual may still make mistakes but is aware of how to correct them.
- 🔆 Unconscious competence: At this final stage, individuals have internalized the knowledge or skills, and they can perform the task without consciously thinking about it. The skill becomes almost automatic and can be performed without effort or conscious thought.

The four stages of competence can be useful for individuals who are seeking to develop new skills or knowledge as it helps them understand the learning process and what to expect as they progress.

Additionally, it can be helpful for trainers or educators to keep these stages in mind when designing training programs or teaching materials.

The Four Stages of Competence Related to Business

The four stages of competence can be related to business in several ways, as they apply to learning and development in the workplace. Here are some examples:

Employee training: Businesses often provide training programs to help employees develop new skills or improve existing ones. Understanding the four stages of competence can help trainers design effective training programs that take into account the learners' current level of competence and help them progress to the next stage.

Performance management: The four stages of competence can also be useful in performance management. Managers can use this model to assess an employee's current level of competence and determine what kind of support or training they may need to improve their performance.

Career development: Employees can use the four stages of competence to guide their own career development. By identifying areas where they lack competence, employees can seek out training or mentorship opportunities to improve their skills and advance in their careers.

Change management: When businesses undergo significant changes, such as a new software implementation or organizational restructuring, employees may need to learn new skills or adapt to new processes. The four stages of competence can help managers understand how employees may react to these changes and develop strategies to support them through the learning process.

Overall, the four stages of competence can be a valuable framework for businesses to understand and support the learning and development of their employees, which can ultimately lead to improved performance and productivity.

How can the four stages of competence be related to entrepreneurship?

The four stages of competence can also be related to entrepreneurship in several ways, as they apply to the process of starting and running a new business. Here are some examples:

- Identifying business opportunities: Entrepreneurs may start in the first stage of unconscious incompetence, where they are unaware of a specific opportunity or industry. As they become more aware and seek out information, they move into the second stage of conscious incompetence, where they recognize their lack of knowledge or experience in a particular area.

- ☀ Developing skills and knowledge: As entrepreneurs move into the second and third stages of conscious incompetence and conscious competence, they acquire the skills and knowledge needed to run their business. This may involve learning about marketing, finance, operations, or other aspects of the business.

- ☀ Building a team: As entrepreneurs move into the third and fourth stages of conscious competence and unconscious competence, they may begin to build a team to support the business. This can include hiring employees or contractors with specific skills, such as marketing or accounting.

- ☀ Scaling the business: Once the business is established, entrepreneurs may need to continue learning and adapting to new challenges in order to scale the business. This may involve identifying new markets, developing new products or services, or implementing new systems or processes.

Overall, the four stages of competence can be a useful framework for entrepreneurs to understand their own learning and development process, as well as the skills and knowledge needed to start and grow a successful business.

By recognizing their own areas of incompetence and seeking out resources to improve their skills, entrepreneurs can increase their chances of success.

How can the 4 stages on competence relate to personal development and self-improvement?

The four stages of competence can also be related to personal development and self-improvement, as they apply to the process of learning and growing as an individual. Here are some examples:

- ☀ Identifying areas for personal growth: Like with entrepreneurship, individuals may start in the first stage of unconscious incompetence, where they are unaware of their own shortcomings or areas for improvement. As they become more self-aware and seek out feedback or guidance from others, they move into the second stage of conscious incompetence, where they recognize their lack of knowledge or skill in a particular area.

- ☀ Developing skills and knowledge: As individuals move into the second and third stages of conscious incompetence and conscious competence, they acquire the skills and knowledge needed to improve themselves. This may involve learning about new subjects, practicing new habits or behaviors, or seeking out mentorship or coaching.

- ☀ Integrating new habits or behaviors: As individuals move into the third and fourth stages of conscious competence and unconscious competence, they begin to internalize their new habits or behaviors. This may involve making conscious efforts to apply their new knowledge or skills until they become automatic and natural.

- ☀ Sustaining personal growth: Once individuals have achieved a certain level of personal growth, they may need to continue learning and adapting in order to sustain their progress. This may involve seeking out new challenges or opportunities for growth, or actively practicing and maintaining their new habits or behaviors.

The four stages of competence can be a helpful framework for individuals who are seeking to develop new skills, behaviors, or habits.

By understanding the learning process and recognizing their own areas of incompetence, individuals can take intentional steps towards personal growth and self-improvement.

What have the four stages of competence and the "conscious competence" model been useful and helpful with in people's lives?

The four stages of competence and the "conscious competence" model have been useful and helpful with many aspects of people's lives. Here are some examples:

- ☀ Learning new skills: The model has been widely used in educational settings to help learners understand the process of acquiring new skills or knowledge. By understanding the stages of competence, learners can approach new subjects with greater awareness and intentionality, and be more effective in their learning.

- ☀ Career development: The model has also been used in career development to help individuals identify areas for growth and development. By recognizing their own areas of incompetence, individuals can seek out training, mentorship, or other opportunities for skill-building and career advancement.

- ☀ Personal growth: The model has been used in personal development and self-improvement to help individuals identify areas where they can improve themselves. By understanding the learning process, individuals can approach personal growth with greater awareness and intentionality, and be more successful in making lasting changes.

- ☀ Communication and teamwork: The model has been used in communication and teamwork training to help individuals understand their own communication style and how to work effectively with others who have different styles. By

96

recognizing their own competence and the competence of others, individuals can communicate more effectively and collaborate more productively.

In general, the four stages of competence and the "conscious competence" model have been useful and helpful with a wide range of personal and professional development goals.

By understanding the learning process and being intentional about their growth and development, individuals can be more successful in achieving their goals and living fulfilling lives.

The Practice of Living a Self-Directed Life

Once you begin to think of what I am sharing with you here as a practice, one that must be nurtured and molded to fit your beliefs, values, and goals, you're on the right track to changing your life by being open to a more self-directed experience.

In every moment, we each have the moment of decision in front of us to choose what we will say, how we will feel, and what action may be most appropriate

Instead of life happening *to* us, we take full responsibility for being a co-creator in the process. This shift will empower you to connect more deeply with the greatness that lies within you and to live up to your full potential.

I hope that just reading these last few paragraphs over a few times, out loud, and perhaps to someone close to you will make a difference in everything you do and help you to stand a little taller than before.

Chapter Nine

Who Most Resonates with You?

*"Your job is to be the best version of yourself
and then invite others to join you."*

~ Mark Groves

It was found that children as young as three months of age were already predisposed to being attracted to some people, while pulling away from others. During my twenty years of classroom teaching, I experienced children preferring to sit next to one particular child over another, and wanting to be in a certain teacher's class for no discernable reason.

Teachers love to change students around on a regular basis, if for no other reason than to provide everyone in the classroom with a new perspective. If a shy child gets used to sitting next to someone who is more dominant, there is a chance that they will not have the opportunity to express themselves as freely. Or, two students may talk too much during instruction time and miss out on something they need to know.

Much of what I am describing here in terms of preference and affinity for another person is unlearned during our formative years. The adults around us nudge us closer to those people they have an affinity towards, rather than allowing us to choose on our own.

There is nothing inherently wrong or prejudiced in these actions, yet we have all felt at times like someone else was making a choice for us that we would have preferred to make ourself.

As an entrepreneur and marketing strategist, I understand the complexity of choosing the people we wish to work with, while avoiding those with whom we do not wish to spend time with, even virtually.

Finding the people we most resonate with is an important step towards self-direction.

Take Me to Your Leader

We all need to feel connected. Community is important, and as an introvert I did not truly understand this concept until I came online to start my online business in 2006.

Previously, I had worked as a classroom teacher for twenty years, and part-time as a real estate broker and residential appraiser for even longer.

Suffice it to say, my days were filled with more people and activities than you could imagine. I longed for the solitude I thought would come from doing everything from my home office. Little did I realize at that time that it wouldn't take long for me to crave the company and companionship of other humans.

I went to Google for answers to this dilemma, as I had become accustomed to doing in recent years. I typed in phrases like "volunteer activities", "business groups", and "things to do in Santa Clarita" "real estate groups" and then scanned through the results.

At the top of the SERPS (search engine results pages) was an article about the local Rotary Club. I had seen the sign for Rotary all across the country as I'd made road trips over the years. The familiar blue wheel was typically posted on signs when you were entering a new area, along with the images and symbols for other groups and service organizations.

I'd never known anyone who was a member of Rotary, or at least I didn't think so. The meeting was at noon on Wednesday at the Marie Callendar's restaurant near the Interstate 5 freeway onramp.

I showed up about fifteen minutes early and slowly approached the entrance to the room where the meeting would be held. I learned long ago that being punctual would make a difference in how I was perceived by others, and it also showed respect.

I was greeted by very nice people. They asked my name and what I did. I wasn't used to the "What do you do?" question, but answered that I was a former classroom teacher and also a real estate broker and residential appraiser. Then they inquired as to why I had come to visit their Rotary meeting on that particular Wednesday afternoon. I told them that I was new to the community and wanted to get to know more people.

It's funny to think back on now, but their questions were helping me to figure out what I was doing in my new life and how I wished to proceed, now that I was working from home and residing in a new city.

During the next ninety minutes, I met many new people and introduced myself a few more times. I was intimidated by the mayor, surprised to see my new dentist and veterinarian, and more than a little bit outside my comfort zone.

This was not my tribe, and not even my community, yet.

As I was thanking the people at my table and shaking hands with the Club's President and a few others as the meeting concluded, I told myself I would probably not visit this group again.

I left the restaurant through a side exit, and just as my hand slipped off the door's handle and I was reaching into my purse to find my sunglasses, I heard my name being called.

I turned around to see a woman who had introduced herself to me, but with whom I had not had a conversation. She was waving her hand and motioning for me to wait for her.

"Connie, it was so good to meet you today. Will you be coming back next week?"

I hesitated, and in that moment my life flashed in front of me. Smiling, I moved closer to her to answer her question.

"I'm not sure. I'm new to Santa Clarita and just started my business, so I don't know if I have time. It's Mary Ann, right?"

"Yes, Mary Ann Croft. Connie, please promise me that you'll come back when you find the time. We're here every week at the same time. We need you in our Rotary Club. We need your voice, Connie."

How could I refuse an offer like that one, I thought.

"I promise. I'll come back when I can."

And with that, we shook hands and went our separate ways. If she had not come after me as I was leaving that day, and spoke to me in that way, I would have most likely missed out on the most important connections and activities I had ever experienced in my life.

I returned a few weeks later, joined a few months after that, and have now traveled the world with this service organization.

Rotary gave me the opportunity to volunteer in the community and beyond, and without their encouragement and guidance I would not have become a public speaker. I dedicated my first book to them when it was published in 2009, and they were as proud of me as any of my friends or family members.

Reading Your Way to Joy and Success

Readers are leaders and many leaders are readers, or at least that's what the posters I received with my book orders from Scholastic said during my years as a classroom teacher.

I had been a reader as a child, and enjoyed getting lost in stories about people and places and animals and plants.

We tend to be drawn towards stories that allow our mind to work through the personal situations and struggles we are currently and have in the past been dealing with in our own lives. I am sure this is why I loved reading stories about happy families and their pets.

If you have gotten out of the habit of reading, I urge you to come aboard once again. When I came online in 2006 to start my business, I forced myself to stop reading the fiction works of some of my favorite authors. These included Elmore Leonard, Stephen King, John Grisham, and more.

I knew that I needed to give myself a business education, so I limited myself to titles from the great minds in the world of business, and also books from thought leaders I was being exposed to at that time.

The reading was tedious for me at first, so I began listening to the audio versions of these books. Soon, I discovered that the way I could best internalize what these masters were sharing was to listen to the book being read, while also reading along with a digital or printed version of their work.

Copywork - Writing and Journaling to Grow and Change

At some point during elementary school. I decided that I wanted to be a writer. There was a boy name Luke who was known for the stories he wrote, and one day he asked me at recess if I would help him write his next story.

I so wanted to be a part of this, yet I wasn't quite where I needed to be to collaborate on this level. Luke went on to be a great writer and even an actor, and I imagine he also learned a lesson after discovering that not all potential writing partners will work out.

I have now collaborated with and co-authored books with a number of people, including the late, great Geoff Hoff, Dr. Joe Vitale, Pat O'Bryan, and most recently, on two books with the awesome Ellen Finkelstein.

Copywork As a Writing Strategy

Copywork means exactly what it sounds like: You take a piece of great writing, and you copy it down, usually with a pen, but it could also be typed. I recommend writing in long-hand, and verbatim for best results.

As a teacher, it was recommended that we begin each day with copywork. We were to select a passage from something we were currently working on, and have the students copy it exactly as it had been written first thing in the morning.

The truth was that I did not understand this process, and during the twenty years I worked in the classroom I never asked for clarification.

The kids disliked copying something from their textbooks or something else we were working on at that time, and I stopped asking them to do it early on in my career. I viewed this as simply a way for the teachers to have more time to take attendance and prepare for the day, instead of being something beneficial to the students.

Until I left teaching and started my business, I never gave this another thought. Now, I understand the great value in this practice and do it daily for about twenty minutes in the morning. It shifts my thinking away from myself and on to the work of someone I am reading or studying.

I like to copy screenplays, as that has become the focus of my writing projects over the past couple of years. I believe this invaluable to me, as I am able to internalize the different parts of each script that I am not yet proficient in for my own work.

Copywork is simply a technique in writing. The idea is to get better at writing by typing out a piece of writing you like.

Famous writers used copywork practices to develop their own art. Writers like Jack London and Hunter S. Thompson rewrote, by hand, the novels and poems that they admired, such as F. Scott

Fitzgerald's The Great Gatsby, just to get the feeling of what it was like to write in that way.

Copying down what other people have written helps develop the intricate connection between your brain, your pen, and your paper, making the difference in the formation of your words, sentences, and language. It helps with making the tiny details and the nuances of great writing feel like something you're creating yourself, because you are. Or at least, you're mechanically producing good writing with your hand.

You may be asking yourself, why would anyone spend their time writing down other people's words when they could be creating their own?

Historically, people did copywork for practical reasons. They wanted a copy of a book, so they had to copy the book by hand. The Bible, for example, was a popular text to copy, and those who rewrote the Bible found themselves feeling closer to the text itself. It was also a common way to teach school age children how to write, especially at the turn of the 20th century. Homeschooling families continue to employ this practice.

The main reason anyone would spend their time doing copywork, though, was simply to become a better writer by opening their mind to new ways of wordsmithing and using imitation as a way to improve skills.

Subliminally, this practice puts you in the position of thinking and feeling what it's like to make something that you really appreciate. You're using other people's work as a warm up to make something new.

Engaging in this practice of manually transcribing or reproducing existing written works as a means of improving one's writing skills involves carefully studying the structure, style, and language of established authors by copying their work word for word.

Another purpose of copywork is to learn from the masters and gain insights into their techniques and craftsmanship. By immersing oneself in the text, writers can internalize the rhythm, flow, and nuances of great writing. It allows them to understand how sentences are constructed, how paragraphs are organized, and how authors employ vocabulary and punctuation to create impactful prose.

This can be done with various types of literature, including novels, essays, poetry, or even non-fiction works. Writers may choose pieces that resonate with their own writing goals or explore a range of authors to develop a diverse set of skills and perspectives.

Through regular practice, copywork helps writers enhance their vocabulary, grammar, and sentence structure. It can also improve their understanding of narrative structure, character development, and dialogue. Furthermore, by engaging with the work of accomplished writers, aspiring authors can cultivate their own unique voice while honing their writing abilities.

It is important to note that while copy work can be a valuable exercise for growth and learning, it is crucial to respect copyright laws and use the transcribed work for personal development purposes only.

The intention behind copywork is not to plagiarize but to employ imitation as a means of skill improvement. It subconsciously places the writer in a state of understanding and appreciation, enabling them to approach their own creations with greater insight. Other people's work serves as a warm-up, setting the stage for the creation of something entirely new.

To reiterate, here are the benefits of using copywork to enhance one's writing skills:

- ☀ Enhances Writing Mechanics: Copywork serves as an exercise in honing fundamental writing mechanics. By carefully transcribing established works, writers develop their spelling, punctuation, and grammar skills. This meticulous attention to detail helps cultivate an intuitive understanding of sentence structure, paragraph organization, and overall composition.

- Expands Vocabulary: Copying the work of accomplished authors exposes writers to a rich and diverse range of vocabulary. They encounter new words, idioms, and phrases, expanding their linguistic repertoire. This expanded vocabulary can then be applied to their own writing, enabling them to express ideas more precisely and eloquently.

- Develops a Sense of Style: Through copywork, writers gain insight into various writing styles and techniques. By immersing themselves in the words and sentences of respected authors, they absorb the rhythm, tone, and voice unique to each writer. This exposure helps them identify and cultivate their own writing style, incorporating elements they find appealing while developing their own distinctive voice.

- Improves Sentence Structure and Flow: Copying well-crafted sentences helps writers internalize the art of constructing clear and coherent prose. They learn how to create smooth transitions between ideas, vary sentence lengths, and use punctuation effectively. As a result, their own writing becomes more polished, engaging, and easier to read.

- Deepens Appreciation for Literature: Engaging with celebrated works through copywork fosters a deeper appreciation for literature. Writers gain a firsthand understanding of the craft behind masterful storytelling, character development, and thematic exploration. This enriched understanding can inspire them to strive for excellence in their own writing.

- Heightens Attention to Detail: Copywork demands careful attention to the nuances of language and style. Writers become more attuned to the subtleties of word choice, metaphor, symbolism, and imagery. This heightened attention to detail translates into their own writing, allowing them to create more vivid and evocative descriptions.

- ☼ Builds Confidence: As writers engage in copywork and witness their progress, their confidence grows. The act of reproducing high-quality writing helps them realize that they are capable of producing work that matches the caliber of their favorite authors. This confidence boost encourages them to take risks, experiment with their own writing, and strive for excellence.

- ☼ Encourages Deep Reading: Copywork necessitates a close reading of the text being transcribed. Writers must comprehend the meaning, context, and intent behind the words. This practice strengthens their ability to analyze and interpret texts, enhancing their overall reading comprehension skills.

- ☼ Internalizes Narrative Structures: By copying various genres and forms of writing, writers gain a deeper understanding of narrative structures. They observe how authors craft engaging beginnings, build suspense, create compelling plot arcs, and deliver satisfying conclusions. This knowledge can then be applied to their own storytelling, making their narratives more captivating and well-structured.

- ☼ Provides a Path for Revision and Editing: Copywork can also serve as a valuable exercise for revising and editing. Writers can compare their transcriptions to the original texts, identifying areas for improvement. This practice trains them to recognize and rectify weaknesses in their writing, ultimately enhancing their self-editing skills.

As you can see, copywork offers numerous benefits for writers. It refines writing mechanics, expands vocabulary, develops style, improves sentence structure, deepens appreciation for literature, cultivates attention to detail, builds confidence, encourages deep reading, internalizes narrative structures, and provides a path for revision and editing. By engaging in this deliberate practice, writers can develop their skills, find inspiration, and ultimately grow as proficient and accomplished wordsmiths.

Chapter Ten

Storytelling Your Way to Success

"One's loyalty has to be to the love of storytelling. And your stories follow you the rest of your life, so one shouldn't produce stinkers out of spite."

- J. Michael Straczynski

I firmly believe that we must take the time and make the effort to activate the greatness that is already within us. How do we achieve this lofty goal? It begins with storytelling and by this, I mean the stories we share with others, as well as the stories we tell ourselves.

Stories are the details and specifics that you tell yourself over the course of your life. They are often based on assumptions, though there can be some truth behind them. In essence, you are basically living in a thought-driven reality.

Your experience in the world is determined by your thoughts. These thoughts impact the way that you feel, the beliefs you embrace, the choices you make, and in turn, by the actions you take and the results you achieve.

We all have different experiences in life, and these contribute to personalized thought patterns, behaviors, and beliefs. These thought patterns cause us to live in our own personalized world, as we navigate life based upon the stories in our mind. I learned this as thoughts lead to feelings, which then become our beliefs, leading us to take actions which lead to the results we experience every day. This flow chart approach and explanation has made a difference in my life.

We must all focus on shifting our thoughts first, which leads to improved feelings, and this changes our beliefs. Once we feel better and believe that we are worthy and capable and that anything is possible in our lives, we take different actions and experience incredible results.

I realize I am reiterating what I am sharing with you here, but I want to make sure you can understand these concepts from a few different perspectives and finally find some part of this that resonates with you in a way that will make a difference in your life.

So, what do these stories you have created for yourself and will project to others around you look like? Common examples of stories you may tell yourself each day include:

"I'm just not good enough."

"I'll never succeed."

"I'm not good at this."

"Someone else deserves this, instead of me."

"I'm too old to start now."

"I should give up."

You'll see that there is a common theme here. Most of the stories we tell ourselves on a daily basis are negative. The mind tends to cling on to negativity much more than it does to positivity. However, there are positive examples too. These include:

"I've got nothing to lose by giving this a try."

"If they can do it, so can I."

"I will work this out."

"I have life experience that will make a difference."

"I deserve to achieve this goal."

If you have a more positive mindset, you are going to tell yourself more positive stories. If you're stuck in a negative mindset on the other hand, your stories will be predominantly negative too.

The stories you tell yourself are basically the thoughts that you have throughout the day. But where does this internal monologue come from? And how will our stories lead to a life that is more resonant with the way we wish to live? Finally, will storytelling make a difference in the way we perceive the world around us, and the way we are perceived by others as we strive to live a more self-directed life?

Why We Have an Internal Monologue

Our internal monologue is partly controlled by a type of brain signal known as corollary discharge. Its purpose is to help you identify the different sensory experiences that occur internally and externally.

This signal helps you to hear your voice as you think, blocking out external stimuli. You can also use it to organize your thoughts when you can't speak out loud.

Another purpose for our internal monologue is to use it to answer questions that we ask ourselves. It can help to identify potential solutions to the problems we face, or make them sound worse depending upon whether you have a positive or negative inner monologue.

These are some of the main reasons why we have that inner voice, and how it can help in our daily lives. One quote, from the late Wayne Dyer is one that I have incorporated into my internal monologue. It goes like this…

"When you change the way you look at things, the things you look at change."

Does Everyone Have an Inner Monologue?

While most of us do have an inner monologue, not everybody hears their own voice or has an inner narrator. Experts aren't sure why this is, but there is a theory that it could be down to how the dorsal stream develops. This is basically the language tract within the brain.

If you can't hear your inner voice, that doesn't necessarily mean that you don't have an internal monologue. Rather than hearing your monologue, you may see it instead. An example would be rather than hearing your to-do list, you might be able to see it in your mind instead.

For most people, their inner monologue is something they can hear. However, it's important to realize that not everybody does have one, and some may experience it a little differently than others.

So, why does our inner monologue matter and what kind of power can our stories have over our lives?

Why Are the Stories We Tell Ourselves Important?

The stories we tell ourselves are important because they control how we live our lives. They can also have an impact on how we see ourselves and the experiences we have. Let's look at some of the main reasons why the stories we tell ourselves are important.

Stories Can Cloud Our Judgement

All too often, the stories we tell ourselves aren't fully true. They are based on our assumptions and beliefs that have developed throughout the course of our lives. If you believe these half-truths, it's going to severely cloud your judgement.

You will make decisions based upon what you believe to be true rather than what is actually true. Stories can cause us to become ingrained in our thought patterns, making it difficult to see different points of view.

If your judgement is clouded, you won't always make the best decisions.

Stories Stop Us from Going After Opportunities

One of the more harmful effects of listening to the stories we tell ourselves, is that they can stop us from going after opportunities. It could be that you don't seek out promotion opportunities because you feel you aren't good enough. Or you may miss out on life experiences because you aren't confident enough to step out of your comfort zone.

If you don't take advantage of the opportunities that come your way, your quality of life is going to suffer. You won't move forward; instead, you'll be stuck right where you are now. For me, this meant changing my life by resigning my position as a classroom teacher, while also working simultaneously in real estate in favor of coming online in 2006 as an online entrepreneur.

Stories We Tell Ourselves Can Wreak Havoc on Our Mental Health

Mental health issues affect over one billion people worldwide. It's amazing to think that a lot of these issues could be down to the stories we tell ourselves.

If you are constantly narrating negative stories in your head, it's going to increase stress, trigger anxiety, and possibly lead to depression. When you are struggling with your mental health, it's difficult to live a life of contentment.

Our Stories Can Damage Relationships

Another reason the stories we tell ourselves are important is because they can damage our relationships. You may feel like your partner dislikes you, or that your friends find you annoying.

This in turn could lead to you viewing your relationships in a more negative light. You may withdraw from your social circle or begin to resent people in your life due to how you think they view you.

If you want strong, healthy relationships, you'll need to be mindful of the stories you tell yourself, and don't forget about the stories you're sharing directly with the people in your life with whom you want to experience healthy relationships.

Personally, the stories I made up in my mind during my twenties and thirties has little or nothing to do with my reality.

While we can't go back in time, we can make sure to move forward more mindfully.

Storytelling Can Impact Our Physical Health

It isn't just your mental health that is impacted by the stories you tell yourself. Your physical health can also take a hit if you are constantly negative.

Negative stories can increase the amount of stress that we feel. Too much stress is known to drastically impact our health and wellbeing. It affects your relationships, sleep, anxiety levels, and it can even impact your life expectancy.

By focusing on more positive stories, it helps to strengthen the immune system, eliminate stress, and protect both your mental and physical health.

Our Stories Impact Our Future

The things you tell yourself will have a huge impact on your future. They can affect the type of job you do, who you surround yourself with, how you spend money, and the places you go.

Practically every part of your future is determined by the stories you are telling yourself right now. While that can be a scary thought, the good news is you can always change the stories narrated inside your head. This means you ultimately have power over how your future goes.

I highly recommend you add the habit of working on your story to the work and self-care you engage in every day. You are creating a legacy and an oeuvre with every story you tell.

Real Life versus a Story Life

If the way that you feel and act is controlled by the stories you tell yourself, how do you know what is real and what isn't? This can be a huge challenge for those looking to switch from a negative mindset to a more positive one.

The trouble with stories is that we often take them as fact. That is, you don't recognize them as being false, or something your mind made up. This can make it a lot trickier to identify what is real and what isn't.

If you're looking to distinguish between reality and fiction, there are some things you can pay attention to. Here, we will look at the difference between real life and story life, and the key ways to start living in reality rather than a distorted storyline made up in your mind.

What Is Real Life versus Story Life?

Real life relates to things that are actually happening. Story life on the other hand, refers to what you perceive is happening. So, it's facts verses perception. Well, almost!

Your story life can reflect real life, but mostly in snippet form. So, you'll have a grasp of reality, but your story influences how you see the world and the people around you.

If you are living a real life, it means you don't let your inner narrator dictate what you think or feel. You are aware of it, but you can separate it from the truth. People living a real life know who they are, and they are typically a lot happier.

If you are living a story life, you are led by your thoughts and emotions rather than facts. You don't have control over your thoughts and feelings, so they tend to dictate how your life goes. People living a story life usually aren't content with what they have or who they are.

So how can you tell if you are living a real or a story life? Here's a few signs to watch out for…

Fact Checking Your Story

To discover if you are currently living a story life, check the facts. How accurate is your story really? If it tells you that you aren't good enough, what are the facts to back that up?

Now, if you suffer with depression, or you are stuck in a negative story life, you might immediately think of the "facts" to support your theory. However, these facts often aren't facts at all. Instead, they are an extension of your story.

What you will often find is that there are no solid facts to back up most of the negative stories you tell yourself. There may be an element of truth there, but no concrete evidence. If you can't find the facts to back up your story, then you aren't living in real life.

Observations Versus Evaluations

In real life, you make observations about the things you around you. You'll notice things as they are, forming an opinion based on fact. When you tell yourself a story, you'll take a more evaluated approach.

Instead of just observing, you'll create scenarios, opinions, thoughts, and feelings related to what you see. A story life goes much deeper than real life, often working on perceptions rather than what is actually going on.

Another thing you'll notice about stories is that they work on hypothetical scenarios. You will constantly think about things that haven't occurred yet, often getting yourself anxious or stressed out over hypothetical situations.

If you want to start living, really living, then you need to focus on the here and now. Whenever you notice yourself going over a hypothetical event or scenario in your mind, stop. Remember to only concern yourself with what is happening right now.

The Power of Positive Stories

So far, we've covered the negative aspects of the stories you tell yourself. However, did you know they can be used for good?

When narrated correctly, the stories you tell yourself can have a positive influence on your life. Simply by switching the narrative of your story, you could enjoy the fantastic benefits below. I have made a concerted effort to turn my stories into positive reflections that may inspire or motivate others, at least in some small way.

Improved Confidence

While negative stories can tear down your confidence, positive ones can build it up. Repeating positive affirmations in your mind and talking positively about yourself will do wonders for your confidence and self-esteem.

When your stories are positive, you'll grab on to any opportunity that comes your way. Even if you are nervous about the opportunity, you'll go after it anyway because you have self-belief. When you are willing to go after opportunities, you'll get to achieve your goals and potentially better your life.

We all need someone in our corner to back us up. What if that someone could be you? The mind is a powerful thing – it can be your greatest ally or your worst enemy. When you follow a more positive narrative, your mind will soon start to fight your corner.

The great thing about this is that when you are your own cheerleader, you don't rely upon anyone else to make you happy. That gives you a lot of power over your life, and it also stops you from making poor decisions.

If your stories are positive, you are going to feel a lot more satisfied in life. You will see things in a completely different light, feeling calm and relaxed, rather than stressed out and sad. You will also be a lot more grateful for the things that you have, making you feel even more content.

So, if you want to become more satisfied in life, paying attention to the stories you are telling yourself will help.

When you fill the mind with negative stories, it leaves you feeling helpless. Positive stories on the other hand put you firmly back in the steering wheel. You will have the self-belief and confidence to overcome your daily worries, and you won't let the "what if's" leave you feeling insecure or helpless.

When you tell yourself positive stories, it's going to have a positive impact on your mental and physical health.

Mentally, it can help to build confidence, reduce anxiety, and decrease the chance that you will fall into depression. Instead, you will feel happy, content, and fulfilled. You won't spend time stressing about things that haven't occurred yet. The reduction in stress alone is a huge benefit.

Your physical health will improve too. Positivity eliminates stress, or at least greatly reduces it. This is great news for your cardiovascular health, reducing the risk of stroke, high blood pressure, and heart attack.

Studies have also shown that positive people live longer. This is likely down to a boost in immunity. So, if you want better mental and physical health, healthier relationships, and increased confidence, it's time to start changing your story into a more positive one.

By now you should have a good idea of what the stories you tell yourself are and where they come from. Being able to distinguish between real and false stories can help you to avoid listening to that negative narrative and go after new opportunities.

Now that you have a better understanding of the stories you are telling yourself, it's time to figure out if they need to be changed and if so, how to do it.

As an exercise in storytelling, I'd like for you to spend some time and thought in writing responses to the following questions. This will be worth your while, I promise. Be prepared to surprise yourself, and know that feelings and emotions are likely to come up for you during this exercise.

What's your story?

Have you ever shared your story with someone, only to discover later that they judged you for something you revealed to them privately?

How do you know when you are sharing too much with someone? How does that make you feel?

How can you present your story in a more meaningful way than you have in the past?

Think of a story about something that happened to you while you were growing up. How can you reframe the details and the outcome to give you a new, positive outlook and memory of what actually occurred during that time?

Chapter Eleven

Living Your Truth

"Life flows on, within you and without you."

~ George Harrison, from his song
"Within You Without You"

Early on in my online business, a woman with whom I had become acquainted asked me if I could teach and show her how to start an online business. I was quite excited to share what I was learning and doing with my online business, so I agreed to travel to her home once a month to spend time with her.

She lived in Las Vegas, a four and a half hour drive each way from my home in Southern California. Every second or third month she would drive to my house and this went on for a year.

No matter how much time I spent with her, and how detailed my explanations of what she needed to do to have some success, she would take little or no action in between the working sessions we did together.

One day, I took a look at her blog and saw that she was now copying my exact blog posts from my website on to hers, and even recommending the same products and courses I was sharing with my readers, but using her affiliate links instead of mine.

I was hurt and confused more than angry, but I called her up to discuss it. She told me she knew why I was calling and was sorry she had stolen my original writing in this way.

She told me that she didn't think I would mind, and that no one would know anyway.

"But you know. And I know." I waited for her reply.

"I'm sure lots of people do this. It's not such a big deal."

We never spoke again after that day. I did run into her at a marketing event in Las Vegas about two years later. She pretended she hadn't seen me and turned around to go in a different direction.

There is no gray area between a lie and the truth. Every word we utter and action we take makes a difference. Living our truth is the only way to move forward, and a self-directed life is only beneficial if we are truthful to ourself first, and then to others around us.

I worked with a man several years ago who lived in fear of his adult children, his friends, and his business associates finding out that he was gay.

He went out of his way to disguise this fact about himself, but with his every word and action, he was telling the world who he really was on the inside.

I had a chance to speak with one of his daughters a year or so later, and she asked me if I had known. When I answered in the affirmative, she told me that she and her siblings felt like this was the "elephant in the room" that was keeping their relationship with their father from being one based on love, trust, and truth.

Actions Speak Louder Than Words

Living in California most of my life, it wasn't until I was in school in New York during the late 1970s that I realized what New Yorkers thought about Californians.

"You say you're going to do something, then you don't follow through." This was a comment from one of my law school classmates.

"Is that true?" I asked.

"Yes, from my experience and that of others I know. If you aren't sure or don't want to do something, just say that."

I thought about this interaction for years before coming to the conclusion that while it might not be true of everyone in California, it was true of my behavior.

It would be another decade before I committed to doing everything I said that I would do. As you can well imagine, this sure did change my life.

A decade later, I began to learn how my core beliefs and values played into everything I was doing, and not doing in my life. Even though we might imagine ourselves working as a veterinarian or an attorney, as I did when I was young, if these careers are not in alignment with your core beliefs and values, they most likely will not be a good fit. This is another excellent reason to learn more about yourself as you seek to create and live a self-directed life.

Core Beliefs and Values

Core beliefs and values are fundamental principles and convictions that guide an individual's thoughts, actions, and behaviors. They form the foundation of a person's identity and play a significant role in shaping their perspectives, decision-making, and interactions with others.

Core beliefs and values often develop through a combination of personal experiences, cultural influences, upbringing, education, and personal reflection.

Over a decade ago I was introduced to someone whose main focus was helping entrepreneurs and writers to discover their core values and deeply held beliefs so as to better understand how they should move forward with their businesses.

I was so taken by her knowledge in this area, and to her commitment to help others to better know themselves in a way that could have earthshattering results, I invited her to speak at the live marketing event I was hosting. I do these conferences twice each year and it seems like the right people always show up just at the right time.

Core beliefs are deeply held notions about oneself, others, and the world. They are often formed early in life and can be difficult to change. They can encompass various aspects, such as beliefs about one's worth, abilities, trust in others, and the nature of reality. For example, a person may hold core beliefs such as "I am capable and worthy of success" or "People are inherently good."

Values, on the other hand, represent principles or standards that individuals consider important and strive to uphold. They reflect what individuals believe is right, ethical, and desirable. Values guide behavior and help individuals make choices aligned with their principles. Common examples of values include honesty, integrity, compassion, fairness, respect, and personal growth.

While core beliefs and values are similar, core beliefs are more focused on cognitive aspects and personal identity, while values emphasize behavioral aspects and moral judgment. Both core beliefs and values are deeply ingrained and tend to influence how individuals perceive the world, interact with others, and make decisions. They provide a framework for understanding oneself and others and can shape one's overall worldview and life choices.

Here are some examples of core values and beliefs that individuals may hold:

- Integrity: Upholding honesty, ethics, and moral principles.
- Respect: Valuing the worth and dignity of oneself and others.
- Responsibility: Taking ownership of one's actions and obligations.
- Equality: Believing in fairness and treating all individuals with equal consideration.
- Empathy: Understanding and sharing the feelings of others.

- ☀ Compassion: Demonstrating care and kindness towards others in need.

- ☀ Authenticity: Being genuine and true to oneself.

- ☀ Open-mindedness: Being receptive to new ideas, perspectives, and experiences.

- ☀ Resilience: Bouncing back from challenges and adversity.

- ☀ Collaboration: Valuing teamwork, cooperation, and working harmoniously with others.

- ☀ Trustworthiness: Being reliable, trustworthy, and dependable.

- ☀ Personal Growth: Commitment to continuous self-improvement and development.

- ☀ Environmental Stewardship: Caring for and protecting the environment.

- ☀ Justice: Believing in fairness, equality, and just outcomes.

- ☀ Faith: Holding strong religious or spiritual beliefs.

- ☀ Freedom: Valuing personal liberty and autonomy.

- ☀ Family: Prioritizing the well-being and support of family members.

- ☀ Education: Recognizing the importance of learning and intellectual growth.

- ☀ Health and Wellness: Valuing physical, mental, and emotional well-being.

- ☀ Innovation: Encouraging creativity, originality, and the pursuit of new ideas.

It's important to note that these examples are not exhaustive, and that individuals will have unique core values and beliefs that are meaningful to them. Also, keep in mind that core values and beliefs can vary significantly from person to person and can be influenced by cultural, religious, and personal factors.

Someone's core values and beliefs play a crucial role in their ability and willingness to seek to live a self-directed life. Here's how they are related:

- ☀ Clarity of Purpose: Core values and beliefs provide individuals with a clear sense of purpose and direction. They help define what matters most to them and guide their choices and actions. By aligning their decisions and goals with their core values, individuals can live a life that is true to themselves and their aspirations.

- ☀ Autonomy and Decision-Making: Core values and beliefs empower individuals to make autonomous decisions. They serve as a compass for navigating life's choices, enabling individuals to assess opportunities, weigh options, and make decisions that align with their principles. This autonomy allows individuals to take ownership of their lives and shape their own path.

- ☀ Authenticity and Self-Expression: Core values and beliefs encourage individuals to live authentically. When individuals stay true to their core values, they are more likely to express their genuine thoughts, feelings, and desires. They are less swayed by external pressures or societal expectations, allowing them to lead a self-directed life that is in harmony with their authentic self.

- ☀ Personal Fulfillment: Living a self-directed life means pursuing what brings personal fulfillment and satisfaction. Core values and beliefs provide a framework for identifying and pursuing activities, goals, and relationships that align with one's authentic desires and values. By living in alignment with their core values, individuals can experience a greater sense of purpose, meaning, and fulfillment in their lives.

- Resilience and Adaptability: Core values and beliefs serve as a foundation of strength and resilience during challenging times. They provide a sense of identity, stability, and motivation to overcome obstacles and adapt to change. When faced with difficult decisions or unexpected circumstances, individuals can rely on their core values to guide them and navigate through uncertainty.

- Self-Empowerment: Living a self-directed life requires a sense of self-empowerment. Core values and beliefs empower individuals to take responsibility for their choices and actions. They provide a sense of control and agency over one's life, enabling individuals to proactively shape their circumstances and pursue their goals in alignment with their values.

As you can see, core values and beliefs are the guiding principles that enable individuals to live a self-directed life. They provide clarity of purpose, autonomy in decision-making, authenticity in self-expression, personal fulfillment, resilience, and self-empowerment.

By honoring their core values and beliefs, individuals can lead a life that is true to themselves, their aspirations, and their intrinsic motivations. You deserve this, and you will find that you feel inspired, motivated, and empowered to move forward in your life by shining a light on the greatness that lies within you each day.

What's Next?

The Focus and Actions of a Self-Directed Life

Walk around feeling like a leaf. Know you could tumble any second. Then, decide what to do with your time.

- Naomi Shihab Nye, from "The Art of Disappearing"

Knowing and doing are two entirely different things, as you may already be aware of in your life experience. In order to become and live what we believe to be the best path for what we resonate with and know we would like to achieve; we must commit to a single focus and massive action.

I did this when I made the conscious decision to come online as an entrepreneur and marketer in 2006, and again just a few years later when I committed to taking my writing to the next level.

You alone must decide what works for you. I have known too many people throughout my lifetime who have allowed others to direct them as to the work they will do, where they will live, and how they will spend their time.

They choose to stay in relationships that do not serve them and may even be harmful in one or more ways. They stay at a job that no longer makes sense for their goals, dreams, and level of knowledge and expertise. And, they give up on the things that once made their heart sing, in favor of not rocking the boat or disrupting the status quo.

I know a lot about this topic because it describes the life I chose to live until I was about to celebrate my 50th birthday. During this time in my life, I sought out the people, books, situations, and events that would take me from where I was at that time – believing I was a victim of my circumstances and that I did not deserve a different, better life – to a life filled with hope, possibility, and opportunities that were mine for the asking and doing.

It was as though I had won the spiritual lottery and since that time, I have made sharing what I now know and have continued to experience with others my life's work.

And I am using the term *work* here to mean the highest and best use of your time, where you serve those around you with your ideas, thoughts, and actions.

I want this for you, even if you and I have never met and live on opposite sides of the planet. You deserve the very best life has to offer, and it is all waiting for you on the other side of the self-directed life you will experience.

Chapter Twelve

When the Student Becomes a Master

"Every exit is an entry somewhere else."

~ Tom Stoppard

During my first year as an entrepreneur with an online business, a woman with whom I was in a Mastermind asked me if I would mentor her as she built and grew an online business of her own.

When I told her I was still learning myself, she said that because I was already making some money online, I was fully qualified to help others do the same. She also stated that her belief was that at some point in everyone's life, the student becomes the teacher and has the potential to become a master.

On that day, I shifted my thinking and belief system and became empowered around this topic. It fell in line with my core beliefs and values in the areas of serving and teaching. Also, I created a new precept in my mind that would be worth millions of dollars in income over the next several years.

This precept was that anyone can become a profitable online entrepreneur, if only they are willing to become an ongoing student of the process and to put in the work required to achieve their goals around time freedom and financial independence.

If you feel you are ready to make the leap from student to master, and are willing to do the added work that will be necessary, then this chapter will be meaningful, and possibly quite profitable for you.

Stay focused and positive, knowing that the life you are reaching for is almost like a parallel universe to where you are at this moment in time. You have so much to offer the world, so isn't it about time you stepped up to the plate and announced your goals and intentions?

Stepping Into Your Power

During the late 1980s, I became involved with technology in new and exciting ways, to the point that I was beginning to use it in almost every area of my life.

I was working simultaneously as a classroom teacher and also part-time as a real estate broker and residential appraiser, and in both cases the topic of computers was always top of mind.

We were in an exciting period of history, where everyone was being asked to embrace something that few could wrap their minds around at the time.

In 1984 I had a Kaypro portable computer. There were two floppy disks, no hard drive, and a tiny screen with amber text and no images.

Yet, as primitive as this sounds, I learned everything I could about how to use it, and soon I was getting listing appointments with people who wanted to sell their home and were impressed by someone who was on the cutting edge of technology.

The following year someone loaned me their IBM computer, and already the learning curve had the potential to pass me by and leave me behind. Then, a year later I purchased a Hyundai desktop computer that came with the newest version of Microsoft's MS-DOS operating system. I waved the flag of surrender, but was not willing to give up my interest in using computers as tools for the future.

That's when I joined a computer user's group that met twice a month, on the second and fourth Thursday, at a public library almost twenty miles from where I lived.

The people in this group would prove to be invaluable to me as I navigated the waters of technology in a row boat without an oar. Instead of getting lost in the sea of terminology, software, hardware, and HTML code, I had my own personal life jacket that not only kept me afloat, but also allowed me to stretch my mind beyond the limits I thought were possible.

Over the next two decades, I grew along with the other members. I was empowered in a way I hadn't previously experienced in my life, and this benefitted me personally, professionally, and spiritually.

By 2005, I had begun my journey of personal growth and self-improvement. I was learning so much, and so quickly so I'm sure I talked about it to everyone who would listen.

Sone of these people who was willing to engage me in conversations about my new experiences was a woman in the computer user's group named Dottie Blake.

Dottie worked in an office, but I don't believe she ever gave us more details. I knew that she did not like the job, but she said she had to pay her bills and I could relate to that.

One Thursday I came into our meeting room and someone motioned for me to hurry over to join the conversation. As I moved in closer, I heard Dottie say,

"So, I've given notice at work and my last day is tomorrow. I'm moving to Ventura to be closer to the ocean. And it's all because of what Connie said to me."

With that, I emitted an audible gasp and then all eyes were on me.

"What did I say, Dottie? I didn't tell you to quit your job and move away. What happened?"

Over the next ten minutes, Dottie recounted a conversation she and I had had the previous month, and I nodded as she shared exactly what I had said to her, almost verbatim.

135

I had told her that life was too short to live it in a way that isn't congruent with who we are. We must learn to create a lifestyle of our own design, and one in which we have the best chance of true joy and happiness. I'd also shared that we must not engage in work that is not fulfilling to our purpose, for if we do, we are taking that work away from someone else for whom it is better suited.

There was more… lots more. On that evening I finally acknowledged what I already knew deep down inside: My mindset had shifted and I could never go back to the place where my thinking had previously resided.

I was ready to follow my own advice, and within a year I had resigned from my classroom teaching job at the end of that school year, and given away my best, long-time real estate clients to others who could better serve them in ways I could no longer promise to do. I was now vibrating at a higher frequency, and I wouldn't have turned back, even if that had been within the realm of reasonable possibilities.

Tuning Into and Relying Upon Your Intuition

Let's return to a discussion of core values and beliefs, and one that I introduced in the previous chapter. Intuition can play a significant role in core values and living a self-directed life. My own intuition continues to grow, and at this point my family members on two continents are used to this new way of looking at and thinking about our lives.

Even though I take action regularly, it is always inspired action. When you're a writer and have your own business, you may truly live a lifestyle by design, giving you the freedom to lay out your schedule in a way that inspires, motivates, and empowers you to allow the greatness that lies within you to manifest.

Here's how intuition relates to these aspects of living a self-directed life:

- Alignment with Inner Knowing: Intuition often represents a deep inner knowing or sense of what feels right or authentic to an individual. It can serve as a compass that helps individuals align their choices and actions with their core values. By listening to their intuition, individuals can make decisions that resonate with their true selves and lead to a more self-directed life.

- Recognizing Value Alignment: Intuition can help individuals quickly assess whether a situation, opportunity, or relationship aligns with their core values. It can provide a sense of resonance or dissonance, guiding individuals to make choices that are in harmony with their beliefs and principles. Intuition helps individuals identify experiences that support their self-directed journey.

- Navigating Uncertainty: Intuition can be particularly valuable in situations where there is limited information or uncertainty. It can provide individuals with subtle cues, gut feelings, or hunches that help guide their decisions. When faced with complex choices, individuals can tap into their intuition to access their deep-seated values and make choices that are true to themselves.

- Amplifying Authenticity: Intuition can act as a powerful tool for expressing authenticity. It helps individuals connect with their inner wisdom and make choices that reflect their genuine desires, passions, and strengths. By trusting their intuition, individuals can live in alignment with their core values, expressing their authentic self in their actions and interactions.

- Personal Growth and Self-Discovery: Intuition can lead individuals on a path of self-discovery and personal growth. By paying attention to their intuitive insights, individuals can uncover new aspects of themselves, explore uncharted territories, and expand their understanding of their core values. Intuition can guide individuals towards opportunities that foster their self-directed development.

☀ Trusting Inner Guidance: Living a self-directed life often involves trusting oneself and making choices based on one's own judgment. Intuition plays a vital role in developing this self-trust. By honing their ability to listen to and trust their intuition, individuals can cultivate self-assurance and confidence in their decision-making, allowing them to live a life that is more self-directed.

It's important to note that while intuition can be a valuable guide, it should be used in conjunction with critical thinking and consideration of other relevant factors. Balancing intuitive insights with rational analysis can help individuals make well-rounded decisions that align with their core values and lead to a more self-directed and fulfilling life.

Embracing the Change You See in Others

Life can be difficult at times. Even under the best of circumstances, situations arise that require us to step up in a way we may feel we aren't yet ready to do.

If you're a child, this can be an even more daunting task. But as humans, we are in a constant state of change, so we must learn to embrace it.

I loved watching my students change during the year we were together in the classroom. Because it was a year around calendar, we started together on July 1st and the school year was finished on June 30th of the following calendar year.

During our months together, I knew that we would take on the hard questions and situations together.

Earlier, I discussed what it was like to work with children who did not yet understand that they were a work in progress, in the present moment and forever after.

On the first day of school, I would ask the class as a whole to write down in their journal the three things they wanted to get out of the school year, what their expectations were on this day, and how I could play a part in their physical and mental transformation.

Yes, I agree that these are pretty lofty ideas and concepts for people who have not yet celebrated their twelfth birthday. But it would not have been fair of me to simply go through the assigned lessons with them each day, and to not touch upon the harder questions and issues that would affect their lives in such an important way.

Many times, when I would visit my students at their homes a parent or older sibling would join in the discussion. It was then that I understood the true meaning of education and of the delicate balance I had to maintain within the work that I did.

My students were from all over the world and from a variety of socio-economic situations. I had no right to tell them they were wrong and I was right when it came to anything I was teaching them. I walked the fine line as best I could, learning that gaining respect through loving kindness was the fastest path to success for everyone involved.

Chapter Thirteen

What I Know, So Far

The best people are like water, which benefits all things and does not compete.

- Tao Te Ching by Lao Tzu (Laozi)

Constant, Never Changing... Or Always Evolving

As the quote above states clearly, the best people go with the flow. This does not mean they do not compete and strive to achieve new and more challenging goals, but they do not allow their ambitions to affect them or others in a negative way.

While I was in the classroom teaching, I noticed that children's personalities are pretty well set at an early age. For fourteen of my twenty years as a classroom teacher, I taught 5th and 6th graders, meaning that they were between ten and twelve years of age.

My observations took me back to my own childhood. By the time I was eleven or twelve I knew that I wanted to be a writer and a veterinarian. I loved animals of all kinds and enjoyed listening to, reading, telling, and sharing stories of all kinds.

Although I took limited action with my writing, I was an avid reader. And my mother and I had only two dogs and several cats throughout these years, I did volunteer at the local zoo, Crandon Park, for two years while we were living in south Florida.

Children in my classroom were already set in their ways by the time they got to me, so I made it a goal to point out their talents and interests and to encourage them to pursue the ones that stood out to them. They also began to dream and plan out loud, something that was a new concept to them. Over the years I had future football and basketball players, artists, musicians, writers, doctors, lawyers, and teachers in my classes.

If only I had taken further steps to ensure their success in a more significant way, but instead of beating myself up over what I didn't do, I focus on what I was able to accomplish during that twenty-year period of my life.

While we may take a snapshot of our current station in life and believe we will never change, the truth is that we are all constantly evolving into a new version of our former self. These changes are too subtle to be noticed, yet a look back at an old photograph proves this out. And if you have ever looked through a book or listened to a piece of music you are familiar with and considered to be a favorite and shook your head as to what you must have been thinking back then, you understand what I'm referring to here.

Perspective Over the Decades

My life perspective has shifted, marginally in some areas and dramatically in others throughout my lifetime. This is to be expected.

At every age and stage of our life, we are comparing, analyzing, and preparing for what is to come. The weather cools down and we put away our lighter-weight clothing and comforter. Our car needs one more repair and we find ourselves asking the neighbor how she likes her vehicle, in hopes of finding greener grass somewhere else.

I have found the best hedge against shifting our perspective for no good reason and just because, is to journal alone and mastermind with others.

A journaling practice allows you to create a running dialogue with yourself, and one in which you can look back on to be reminded of what you were thinking in the past.

Masterminds continue to be the way I check myself against what others in my business are thinking about and doing. Find a Mastermind to join, or start one of your own!

Work Ethic: Take Responsibility and Make It Happen

When you live a self-directed life, the precept is that you can make anything happen that you choose to include as a part of your life experience.

This does not mean that you aren't looking to God, the universe, or to the higher power you accept and believe in for guidance. Instead, this can mean that you are taking a more wholistic approach to figuring out your life in terms of your choices, beliefs, and actions.

I will admit that my work ethic left much to be desired as a younger person. I became aware of this as I was starting my business as an online entrepreneur, marketer, and author during 2006.

So much so, that I wrote and published a book about my experiences, and how anyone may emulate these proven strategies, titled *Rethinking the Work Ethic: Embrace the Struggle and Exceed Your Own Potential*.

Punctuated Equilibrium

The path towards a self-directed life is an evolutionary one. Most people understand evolution as a slow, steady process: Incremental changes that stack up over millions of years. But there's another theory, called punctuated equilibrium, that proposes that things pretty much stay the same for a long time, and then there's a sudden jump.

While punctuated equilibrium is a theory primarily used in the study of evolutionary biology, some people have applied the idea to personal growth and self-improvement. The basic concept is that personal growth and development can also occur in fits and starts, rather than as a steady and continuous process.

In this context, punctuated equilibrium suggests that periods of personal growth and development may be punctuated by moments of rapid change or breakthroughs. These breakthroughs can be triggered by various factors, such as major life events, experiences of adversity, or new insights gained through self-reflection or learning.

The periods of stability or stasis in between these breakthrough moments may last for extended periods, during which little personal growth is experienced. However, these periods can be valuable for consolidating previous learning and preparing for the next burst of growth.

The idea of punctuated equilibrium in personal growth and self-improvement emphasizes the importance of taking advantage of opportunities for growth and development when they arise, rather than feeling discouraged by periods of relative stagnation. It also highlights the potential for sudden breakthroughs and encourages individuals to remain open to new experiences and learning opportunities that can facilitate personal growth.

The punctuated equilibrium model proposes that the evolution of a species – humans, in this context - occurs in five stages:

- First Stable State: The species is in a period of relative stasis or stability, during which time there is little evolutionary change.
- Triggering Event: A significant event occurs that disrupts the stability of the species, such as a change in environmental conditions or a genetic mutation.
- Rapid Change: The species undergoes a relatively rapid burst of evolutionary change, which may include the emergence of new traits or the formation of new species.
- Second Stable State: The species returns to a period of relative stability, during which there is once again little evolutionary change.

☀ Repeat: The cycle of stability, triggering event, rapid change, and stability repeats itself over time, as the species continues to evolve.

It's important to note that the duration of each stage can vary widely, and some stages may be skipped altogether depending on the circumstances. Also, the punctuated equilibrium model is not a linear process, and different parts of the species population may be in different stages at the same time.

Thinking back to my own personal growth and evolution during the past two decades, I can now see and understand some of what I experienced by relating it to this model.

My *First Stable State* began around age thirty, when I decided to return to college to earn my teaching credential, and, in turn to step away from real estate and only engage in these activities on a part-time basis.

Although the teaching profession did not appear to be a perfect situation for my needs and expectations, it was a stable career that allowed me to work with children and do something I had always believed was a worthy career goal.

The *Triggering Event* occurred in stages while I was teaching. It began when we went out on strike at the end of my first year and I realized that maintaining my real estate business would make sense for me.

Some years later I would be diagnosed with cancer for the first time, and unable to work in the classroom for the good part of a year. It was during this time that I became more active as a residential real estate appraiser. This work allowed me to make my own hours and not to have to be on call during times when I needed to rest or have treatments and other medical procedures.

The final *Triggering Event* would come for me several years later, when an accident at school required me to have surgery for a torn meniscus on my knee, as well as rotator cuff surgery for my shoulder.

I was out of work for six months and depleted my savings in the process.

It was during this period that I began to pray each day for a way to *"work at home, from my bedroom if necessary, and to meet all of my financial obligations with grace and ease."*

This threw me into the *Rapid Change* stage and I began reaching out to and connecting with people who had gone through a transformation in their life, related to their work and personal growth and development.

Within a few months I had discovered the world of online entrepreneurship and my plan to resign from teaching and give away my long-time real estate clients to people who could better serve them going forward took place.

Soon, I entered my *Second Stable State*, learning as much as I could about writing, marketing, and creating so that my transition from employee and service provider to online entrepreneur would be as smooth as possible.

This cycle of stability, triggering event, rapid change, and stability continues to play out in my life, and I am dedicated to walking this path alongside the people I mentor in my business.

Chapter Fourteen

Your Legacy

"Legacy. What is a legacy? It's planting seeds
in a garden you'll never get to see."

\- Lin-Manuel Miranda

When I first met a man who told me he did something called "legacy planning" with businesses and individuals, I told him that I wasn't familiar with this phrase.

He went on to explain that in its most simplistic state, this referred to a financial strategy that prepares people to bequeath their assets to a loved one or next of kin after death. These affairs are usually planned and organized by a financial advisor.

But this was more of a textbook definition. Legacy planning is a financial strategy used to create a plan for your estate after you die. It may also help mitigate tax issues by giving you more of an understanding and choices between various tax scenarios that could impact your estate or your beneficiaries after your death.

But within the context I'm thinking of here, your legacy will include your oeuvre: a substantial body of work constituting the lifework of a writer, an artist, or a composer. An artist's oeuvre is their total body of work.

Oeuvre can also refer to a single work of art, but it most commonly refers to the collective work of an artist over a lifetime.

Yes, you are an artist, a creative, a thinker whose thoughts, ideas, and actions will change the world. Your goal is to leave your handprint and footprint upon the earth in such a way as to impact people generations into the future.

Lest you are thinking this is too lofty a goal for anyone to have for themselves, let me remind you that your lifetime is the opportunity for you to make a statement that will be included in the permanent records of mankind.

In 1790 Edmund Burke said, "People will not look forward to prosperity who never look backward to their ancestors."

I now think of my legacy as one in which I share my life experiences, beliefs, and perspectives with others through the stories I tell. My writing and my speaking have come to mean everything to me.

Living Up to Your Potential

While I was a teacher, we moved away from decades of filling out report cards for the students by hand, to using a computer program. I helped those who were less tech-savvy than myself, and the new system was admittedly a faster and more proficient way to accomplish this task every twelve weeks.

However, there was one part of the process than none of us liked: In order to add comments to the child's report card, you had to choose from the pre-written ones instead of crafting your own.

No one loves "canned" comments, but when you have no choice, you'll do what you have to in order to get to the place you want to be.

There was a comment I used to write on the report card that went like this: *Not working up to their potential.* This meant, in my thinking that the child was smart and capable, yet not doing the work or making the effort in order to earn better grades.

When this comment, or anything even remotely close was not included in the new software program, I decided to petition the school district to add it. When I reached out to them, I was told to submit my request in writing and someone would get back to me.

Assuming that my letter would end up in the "circular file" I decided to write what I truly thought was an excellent comment for the power that be to consider...

> *Working at or above their potential, in a way that will make a positive difference throughout their remaining years of formal education, and beyond.*

That was what I submitted. A couple of months later I received a letter thanking me for my input, and notifying me that the new comment had been added to the program and would be available to use during the next reporting period.

On that day I realized that I was capable of living up to my full potential, and I stood a little taller from that moment going forward.

Everything Old is New Again

Don't you love it when someone you know discovers something for the first time, and you realize that whatever it is, it has been around for many years?

We have come to expect to experience this regularly with children, so I was surprised when the adults of all ages and backgrounds that I work with in my online business were also finding out things that I had incorrectly assumed were a part of the lexicon and the common knowledge of the people I would continue to encounter throughout my lifetime.

This was when I began to have fun with words and ideas in a way that was new to me.

What if I could share my ideas in such a way that they would be perceived as completely new ones? I do not mean that I would take someone else's idea and simply rewrite it; no, what I am referring to here is the reworking of an idea into something unrecognizable, even to you.

149

My vocabulary had never been as extensive as I wanted it to be, so I took on the role of student once again and proclaimed myself to be a "learner of words and phrases and a wordsmith in training." I now play with words as they relate to my thoughts and ideas, turning myself into a scribe every single day.

And, I search my memory for the words that have flowed through my brain in the past and that I did not take the time with to understand their true and intended meanings.

One of these words in entropy. Two decades ago, I heard a band play at a festival and their name was Entropy. The people I was with that weekend laughed and said it made perfect sense for them to be there because their group's name was a perfect fit. I laughed along with them, but it wasn't until just a few years ago that this memory circled back around to the part of my brain where I was once again reminded of it.

I conducted extensive research into the word and put together a document that clarified this theory for me. Then I wrote about it as part of a new information product I was creating.

People continue to thank me for what I created, and I always remind them that it was not my original idea and that it has been around for ages. Everything old can become new again, if you are willing to do the work to bring it forward in a way that resonates with you.

Drawing Strength from Previous Generations

When Hans came to my family as an exchange student from China in 2012, I was taken by his interest in getting to know and learn from people of all ages and backgrounds.

He explained to us that he had been taught to not only respect his elders, but to learn as much from them as possible to enhance his own life experience. He went on to share that he believed that connecting with people who were alive during generations before he was born could be helpful when attempting to understand and solve problems and issues in the current times.

Yes, wise beyond his years and a thought leader in the making, to be sure. He is currently living in Hong Kong and beginning his career as a human rights attorney.

Hans is not the only person I know who continues to draw strength and gain insight from their ancestors and previous generations.

I have friends who own an insurance business that started with the grandparents who were born at the turn of the century and immigrated to the United States from Ireland when they were young children.

They struggled in a variety of ways and discovered that hard work, a strong work ethic, education, and starting a business would be their pathway to a better life.

The insurance company began in the 1930s, and they committed to having every family member and their spouses learn and work in the business in some capacity.

By the end of World War II, they had relocated to southern California. But they never left behind the lessons they had learned and the ideals and beliefs they held.

When I first met them in the 1980s, they had four generations active in their company and I was left breathless while observing the work ethic they had set for themselves.

I continue to do business with this family and we have now had many conversations around how I chose to emulate many of their habits and productivity strategies and use them to change my life and grow my business.

My recommendation is that you connect with people much older and wiser than yourself. Ask them questions you believe you already know the answers to, and listen closely to how they respond. Writing by candlelight, with pen and paper, on a manual typewriter, or on a keyboard will lead to the same creative result; knowing as much as possible about our history will keep us from making mistakes that do not need to be repeated.

Epilogue

*"Everything we do in our lives is preparing us
for something that will arise in the future; we
don't yet know what that might be.*

~ Connie Ragen Green

This book has been a joy to think about while I am alone, to discuss with others - like-minded or not, to research, and to write. I've often said that writing my books is much like reading someone else's book for the second or third time, in that the concepts and lessons are now familiar.

During the writing of this book, I feel like I grew into more of the person I continue to want to become. We are all works in progress, but witnessing that growth often eludes us.

A few books made the difference for me this time and I will share them with you here.

How to Begin: Start Doing Something That Matters by Michael Bungay Stanier jumped out at me from my bookshelf.

This book has become so important to me and the lessons within its pages now fit me like a comfortable piece of clothing.

Michael encourages us to Set a Worthy Goal; Commit; and Cross the Threshold."

This advice sounds so simple when you first come across it in the first few pages. Yet, how many of us have been willing to take to heart even the idea of setting a worthy goal.

For me personally, I had abandoned the hope of achieving anything important in my life while I was still in my thirties. It would be someone else - someone smarter, younger, better connected, more likable, and someone who was more deserving than I would ever be.

Then the years marched on, and I knew I had to be willing to fail if my life experience was going to improve. I did fail, many times, but I was failing *forward* and learning so much that it was almost a joyous process.

My worthy goal was to leave my life as a classroom teacher and real estate broker and appraiser behind, and to trade it in for my own business on the internet; I committed to this goal when I resigned from the school district at the end of the school year, and gave away my longest and best real estate clients to others who could better serve them going forward; and I crossed the threshold when I turned on my computer and figured out how to start a blog.

And, always remember that although I am suggesting here that you inspire, motivate, and empower yourself to strive to connect with the greatness that lies within you, know that you need not walk alone. It took me decades to understand that people everywhere want others to succeed, and that revelation alone has been something of a revolutionary discovery along my journey.

You also may be wondering how I am coming along with getting back on track with my healthy eating after falling off of my intermittent fasting practice almost a year ago.

I am pleased to tell you that I chose a day to begin again, and have not wavered since that time. I'm losing weight, my A1C and other numbers are returning to normal, and I am feeling energized and focused with a clarity I had all but forgotten was possible. I was self-directing my life once again!

Perhaps my detour in regards to my health was exactly what was needed to give me the ideas I was searching for to share in this book.

Will authors do most anything to share a story they believe has merit and will inspire a new group of readers? Perhaps.

> *"No excuses. Find your voice and tell the*
> *world every morning... I'm back."*

~ Sandy Gallagher

About the Author

Connie Ragen Green is a writer, bestselling author, international speaker, and online marketing strategist who is dedicating her life to serving others as they build and grow successful and lucrative online businesses.

Her background includes working as a classroom teacher for twenty years with the Los Angeles Unified School District, while simultaneously working in real estate as a licensed broker and certified residential real estate appraiser. In 2006, she left it all behind to come online, and the rest is history.

She makes her home in two cities in southern California; Santa Clarita in the desert and Santa Barbara at the beach. In addition to her writing and work online, Connie consults and strategizes with several major corporations and some non-profits, as well as volunteering with groups such as the service organization Rotary International, the Boys & Girls Clubs, the women's business organization Zonta, SEE International, and several other charitable groups.

As the recent recipient of the Merrill Hoffman Award, presented to Connie by the Santa Barbara Rotary Club, being honored with this award has strengthened her resolve to serve others around the world in any way she is able to by using her gifts, talents, and experiences in a positive and sincere manner. Her online business is the vehicle for this and Connie continues to serve entrepreneurs, authors, marketers, and speakers, both new and seasoned.

Made in the USA
Coppell, TX
10 August 2023

20201509R00098